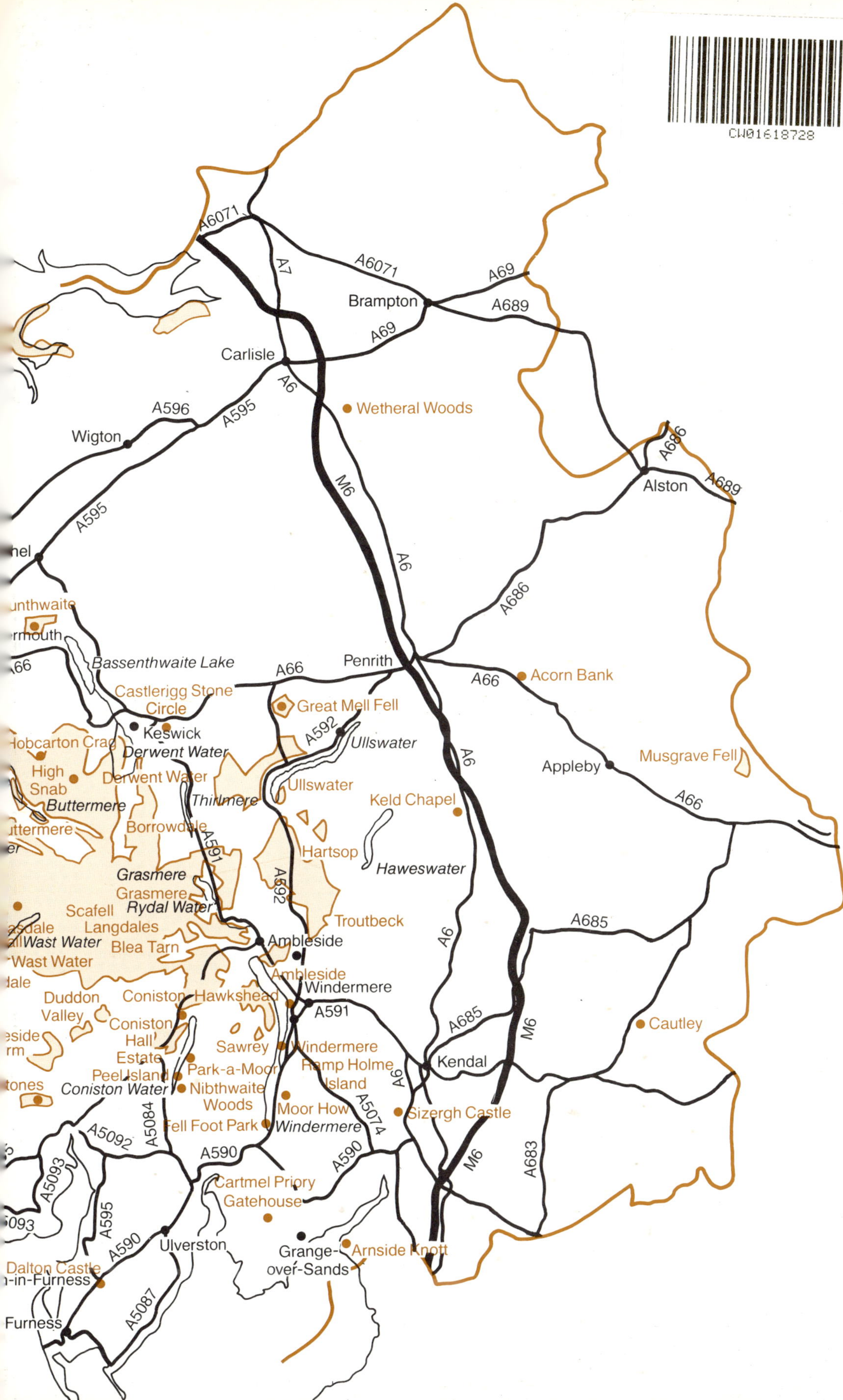

A6071
A7
A6071
A69
Brampton
A689
A69
Carlisle
A6
Wetheral Woods
A596
A595
Wigton
M6
A595
A6
A686
A686
Alston
A689
Bassenthwaite Lake
A66
Penrith
A66
Acorn Bank
Castlerigg Stone Circle
Great Mell Fell
Keswick
A592
Ullswater
Derwent Water
A6
Appleby
Musgrave Fell
High Snab
Derwent Water
Ullswater
Buttermere
Thirlmere
Keld Chapel
A66
Borrowdale
A591
Hartsop
Haweswater
Grasmere
A592
Grasmere
Scafell
Rydal Water
Troutbeck
A685
Langdales
Blea Tarn
Ambleside
A6
Wast Water
Ambleside
Windermere
Duddon Valley
Coniston
Hawkshead
A591
Coniston Hall Estate
A685
M6
Cautley
Sawrey
Windermere
Ramp Holme Island
Kendal
Peel Island
Park-a-Moor
A6
Coniston Water
Nibthwaite Woods
Moor How
A5074
Sizergh Castle
A5092
A5084
Fell Foot Park
Windermere
A590
A590
M6
A683
A5093
Cartmel Priory Gatehouse
A595
A590
Ulverston
Grange-over-Sands
Arnside Knott
Dalton Castle
A5087
Furness

NATIONAL TRUST HISTORIES

THE LAKE DISTRICT

CHRIS BARRINGER

Series Editor Richard Muir

Willow Books
Collins
Grafton Street, London
in association with
The National Trust
1984

Willow Books
William Collins & Co Ltd
London Glasgow Sydney Auckland
Toronto Johannesburg

Barringer, Chris
The Lake District – (National Trust
regional history series)
1. Lake District (England) – History
I. Title II. Series
942.7'8 DA670.L1

Hardback ISBN 0 00 218058 8
Paperback ISBN 0 00 218103 7

First published 1984

Made by Lennard Books
Mackerye End, Harpenden
Herts AL5 5DR

Editor Michael Leitch
Designed by David Pocknell's Company Ltd
Production Reynolds Clark Associates Ltd
Printed and bound in Spain by
TONSA, San Sebastian

Cover Photographs

Centre: Crummock Water

Top left: Castlerigg Stone Circle

Top right: Derwent Water

CONTENTS

9
Editor's Introduction

11
The Shaping of Cumbria
Character of the region;
The story in the rocks;
Climate and the Cumbrian landscape.

22
Prehistoric and Roman Times
Stone Age communities and their domestic remains;
The first monuments;
Roman routes and settlements;
Hadrian's Wall and the west coast forts.

32
After the Romans
The Celtic North-West;
Anglo-Saxon inroads;
Crosses and tombstones of the early Christians.

35
The Norman Period
Origins of the counties – Cumberland, Westmorland and Lancashire;
Norman castles;
The monastic impact;
Parish churches.

44
The Medieval Landscape
Villages and farmsteads;
Power in the parishes;
The 'Records of Kendale';
Pele towers;
The medieval market-place;
Parks and forests.

56
The Statesmen and the Miners
Farming the fells – infield and outfield;
Early industry – iron, copper, lead and slate.

64
The Eighteenth Century
Age of the Picturesque – Wordsworth's 'perfect Republic';
The Cumberland Coalfield and its ports;
Industrial and market towns.

74
The Nineteenth Century
Industrial growth;
Literary visitors;
Expansion in Carlisle;
Railway connections.

85
Cumbria Today
The great conifer debate;
Building the reservoirs;
Tourism and the National Park.

92
Acknowledgments, Further Reading, Index

EDITOR'S INTRODUCTION

Whenever I visit the Lake District in spring, autumn or winter I am always convinced that there cannot be a more beautiful place in all the world. A glance at the atlas tells us that this is a relatively small and compact area, with the Lake District core of Cumbria covering not that much more ground than the built-up area of London.

The atlas also tells us that the main three-thousand-footer peaks of the region are mere pimples in comparison to the Alps, let alone to the Himalayas. But atlases cannot tell us about the character and ethos of the area, and the Lake District has an aura of bigness which defies the cartographical facts. The lakes seem broader, the grey summits loftier and the crags more defiantly vertical than they really are. The deceptions do not end here, and most visitors probably imagine that in these rugged, largely unspoilt and sometimes almost brutal landscapes one is meeting a natural wilderness. Yet in fact the scenery of the Lake District is emphatically man-made. Were it not for the efforts of man the farmer, active here for at least six thousand years, the fells would still be blanketed in pine, hazel and oak. Today, when so many lovely English landscapes have been heedlessly destroyed by modern agriculture, the tough and sometimes impoverished hill farmers are still helping to maintain the lovely scenery of fell pasture, moor and walls which are the essence of the region's charm.

The Lake District was, until the nineteenth century, a remote, neglected and inaccessible part of England. Before the arrival of good communications and tourism it had been home to successive generations of very hardy people: prehistoric peasant farmers, the defenders of small Roman garrisons, Norse and Saxon settlers, monastic tenants and, after the Dissolution of the Monasteries, the doughty farming families of yeomen or 'statesmen' and communities of miners and quarry workers. Each group has left its powerful imprint on the landscape and there is an exceptional legacy of prehistoric and Roman monuments, interesting medieval castles and monastic buildings and a wealth of post-medieval vernacular buildings in stone, as well as plenty of relics to attract the industrial archaeology enthusiast.

It is fitting that the Lake District should be the subject of one of the first volumes in this series of National Trust regional histories, since the Trust manages so many properties in the region and has done so much to conserve its beauty. There are scores of books which delight in the loveliness of the Lake District, but very few which tell the visitor in uncomplicated terms about the creation of the landscape. There are also very few scholars who understand this story as well as Chris Barringer does. He was educated at Ilkley in Yorkshire and at St John's College, Cambridge. Between 1954 and 1965 he was Senior Geography Master at Lancaster Royal Grammar School and, working on the threshold of the Lake District, he could explore every facet of the lake and fell country and develop an understanding of the history of its peripheral towns. This close acquaintance with the region has been regularly renewed since he became Resident Tutor in Norfolk for the University of Cambridge Board of Extra-Mural Studies. Chris Barringer's previous works include a more detailed guide to the geography of the Lake District and a fine landscape history of the Yorkshire Dales.

Richard Muir
Great Shelford, 1983

THE SHAPING OF CUMBRIA

Cumbria is one of the most clearly defined areas of England. It stretches from Morecambe Bay to the Solway Firth and from the Irish Sea to the valleys of the Lune and Eden Rivers. Not only is it a clear-cut geographical area, it is also unique in English landscapes for its combination of lakes and mountains. Local government reforms in 1974 recognized this unity of the 'Lake counties' in renaming Cumberland, Westmorland and parts of Lancashire and the West Riding of Yorkshire under the umbrella name of 'Cumbria'. It is sad to have lost Cumberland and Westmorland as names, and the attractive-sounding 'Lancashire across the sands', but Cumbria has a presence of its own.

Our story begins long before the counties appeared and runs through to modern times and the creation of England's busiest National Park. Other sections discuss the stories of the Lake poets, the Lake artists and writers, and the growth of the Lakes as a favourite holiday area. These themes are, of course, closely related and one may well ask why such a small part of England has come to be so well-known. The 'typical' English scene, perhaps based on perceptions of Stratford-upon-Avon and the Cotswolds, is often portrayed as one of the slow-flowing stream, of thatched cottages grouped near a timeless church and very probably round a village green. The Lake District, the core of Cumbria, has none of these: its streams roar, its cottages are slate-roofed, and its churches, other than those few in market towns, date largely from the nineteenth century.

Perhaps it is in part this very 'differentness' that attracts the traveller. The concept of the Grand Tour, born in the eighteenth century, and later the Gothic Revival movement in architecture, both stimulated educated people to take an interest in new and unusual places. Wordsworth was born in the Lakes and returned to them and so, through him, many more literary and artistic figures were introduced to the region. Painters looking for the Picturesque turned Lakeland vistas into Wagnerian backdrops: Turner, Towne and Harden presented these new scenes for the delectation of new connoisseurs. The railways and the Lakes steamers allowed the *nouveaux riches* of Liverpool, Manchester and Tyneside to buy up the Lakeside estates on Windermere and around Keswick.

Since then, the Lake District has held its own with the cut-price, jet-borne search for the sun. The YHA, school trips, Outward Bound projects, the 'cult' of Peter Rabbit, television films on wildlife and rock climbers, and Ken Russell's version of Wordsworth striding into the mist, have all drawn new groups of visitors to the Lakes. Meanwhile, the M6 has made it possible for holiday-season motorists to reach Ambleside and Keswick in ever-greater numbers – their queues unfortunately matching those which extend out of nearby traditional resorts such as Blackpool and New Brighton. In fact, so successful has the Lake District become as a resort area that its administrators now try to disperse ramblers more evenly and discourage motorists from all seeking to park their cars at the same viewpoint. Perhaps this book can help further those aims by leading walkers and motorists to look beyond the 'honey pots' and discover the host of lesser-known sites when they visit the region, and so enjoy it more fully.

The Story in the Rocks

How far back must we go in attempting to unroll the story of the Lake District? This account will focus on man and his story in the area, but it is also important that the impact of Nature should be understood. Nature's landscape has been much altered by man so that it is not only lake and fell that characterize the Lakes but also the tough stone buildings, the miles of grey stone walls, the bleating of sheep on the fells

The Skiddaw Massif, Ashness Bridge and Derwent Water. The steep but regular slopes of the Skiddaw Slates are cut into Cumbria's oldest rocks.

Oxendale at the head of Langdale shows the 'knobbly' irregular surface produced by the varied rocks of the Borrowdale Volcanic Series.

and the smell of bracken that provide the detail and flavour – and these are all man-made effects. So too are the smell of fish and chips in Ambleside and the din of motor boats on Coniston Water.

Even so, really to appreciate the Lakeland scene we must understand its rocks and physical structure. Cumbria is geologically one of the oldest parts of England: only parts of the Welsh Borders, the Malvern Hills and scattered uplands such as the Wrekin in Shropshire are older.

In Ordovician times, some five hundred million years ago, Cumbria, like North Wales to the south-west and Scandinavia to the north-east, was part of a great structural trough, very much like present-day Indonesia. It was a zone of frequent volcanic activity during which masses of ash and lava were thrown out by volcanoes. The sea in which this activity took place was muddy and thousands of feet of sands and muds were deposited when the volcanoes reached above sea level and their cones were quickly eroded. Major forces of movement in the earth's crust exerted lateral pressure on these deposits or 'sediments' as the crustal 'plates' or great slowly-moving continental landmasses compressed these materials between them. (The same processes are taking place now in India where the 'plate' of the Deccan is squeezing the Himalayan sediments up against the ancient mass of Siberia.) The Cumbrian mountains were thrust upwards to form mountain ranges looking not unlike the modern Himalayas or Alps. The Ordovician sea was inhabited by primitive forms of crabs known as trilobites and by many forms of shellfish, but there were no vertebrate fish and no land plants or animals.

The oldest, that is the lowest, sediments in Cumbria are known as the Skiddaw Slates and they now give rise to distinctive scenery, exemplified by Skiddaw Mountain near Keswick. Because of the later geological history of the region these rocks form a high ridge running south-westwards from Skiddaw very nearly to the coast near Egremont. The slates began as fine-grained sediments laid down in a deep ocean trough and they do not vary greatly in character. Therefore, when the forces of erosion work on them they produce more regular slopes than their successors, the rocks of the Borrowdale Volcanic Series.

The compression between the ancient plates of 'Atlantis', which then lay in the area now occupied by the North Atlantic Ocean, and a less definable plate located where the North European Plain is today, became so severe that the earth's crust was fractured and molten material from the deeper surface layers began either to pour out into

The Silurian rocks of the southern Lake District give lower surfaces with more uniform summit levels. This view is near Broughton-in-Furness.

the sea as lava or to build up volcanic cones as ash. In some outbursts ash fell and volcanic 'bombs' were blown out of the vents to settle in the ash and form rocks known as 'tuffs'. Lava, ash and tuffs make up the Borrowdale Volcanic Series, and the landscape of the late Ordovician period, perhaps four hundred and fifty million years ago, would have been like the volcanic scenery of modern Iceland, Hawaii or Java.

An essential feature of volcanic rocks is their variety, so that any hillside carved into them will reflect these differences within the mass of rock and be irregular and varied in its character. One has only to look at the Langdale Pikes at the head of Langdale Valley or at Borrowdale to see the characteristic broken and knobbly scenery formed on these volcanic rocks. They account for nearly all the highest peaks in the Lake District: Scafell Pike, 3210 ft (977 m), and Helvellyn, 3118 ft (949 m), are the highest.

The volcanic activity died away with a return to muddy seas in which sediments were laid down in Silurian times to form a third major group of rocks known as the Silurian Series. These were laid down some 440–400 million years ago and they contain fossils of vast numbers of shellfish. Like the Skiddaw Slates, they are more uniform in character than the Borrowdale Volcanic Series and thus the landscape that has developed on them, in the southern Lake District in particular, is less dramatic than that of the Central Fells.

Rock laid down in water as sediments, whether as muds or as ash, will be nearly horizontal and the Silurian beds and the Borrowdale Volcanics might be expected to be lying over the older Skiddaw Slates. However, if the comparison with the Alps and Himalayas is continued, the great lateral pressures from the compression by the plates buckled both the muds of the Skiddaw Slates and the volcanic rock of the Borrowdale Volcanics. The pressure compressed and hardened the muds, ashes, lavas and tuffs into rock forms quite different from their original sedimentary nature. Under pressure and heat the mineral constituents of the rocks changed and new ones grew; as a result of these forces the rocks took on their 'slatey' character which was important for their future value to man. This change in the character of rocks is termed their 'metamorphosis' so that they are now known as 'metamorphic rocks': rocks that have been changed.

This phase of mountain building that took place in Silurian and Devonian times about four hundred million years ago is known as the 'Caledonian' period of mountain building, and the mountains of Scandinavia, the Southern Uplands of Scotland, Cumbria and North Wales were all formed in this period.

Just as the forces of erosion are now lowering all existing mountain ranges, so the Caledonian mountains were worn away throughout the Devonian period, some four hundred to three hundred and fifty million years ago.

It is difficult to visualize these very long-term geological processes and, perhaps, it is most difficult of all to understand the next stage in Cumbria's long geological history. The erosion during Devonian times was so complete that the Caledonian mountains were planed right down to a flat surface. This surface was drowned by a warm, lime-rich sea in Carboniferous times (350–270 million years ago). Fish had evolved in Devonian times, as had the first land plants. By the Carboniferous period the seas were rich in corals, fish and amphibians and their remains accumulated to provide the material from which the distinctive white, blocky limestones of the region were formed. Later in the period the sea became shallow and river deltas and creeks filled with forests of giant ferns and conifers from which the coal seams were to form. Hence the term carbon-bearing (carboniferous) is applied to the period. The Carboniferous rocks now stand highest on the west edge of the Pennines at Cross Fell which is 2930 ft (893 m) high. The thickness of the rocks on Cross Fell and the fact that they have been completely worn away from the Central Lake District, and that they occur again on the west coast plain, is a reflection of another major chapter in the geographical story of Cumbria.

A second phase of mountain building, the Hercynian, occurred in late Carboniferous and early Permian times (300–260 million years ago). It was not as dramatic as that of the Caledonian, but the Lake District came to be at the centre of a great structural dome that was thrown up. It was this uplift and doming that exposed the Carboniferous limestone to rapid erosion, so that it was stripped right off the Lake District Fells. One can appreciate this phase very clearly from the minor road to the west of Greystoke Forest and from Knipescar, to the north-east of Haweswater, where the gently tilted limestones can easily be visualized as continuing westwards from the Pennines, high over the present ancient summits. A great fault, or vertical fracture, caused the Eden Valley trough to form at the foot of the Pennine escarpment.

The erosion of the Permian dome took place under conditions of desert weathering, very much like those at work in the American deserts of Colorado and Nevada today. Desert sand dunes and salt lakes filled the Eden Valley and Solway and coastal plains.

A third period of mountain building, known as the 'Alpine' period because it was responsible for uplifting and folding the Alps and beginning perhaps sixty million years ago, seems to have revived the Lake District dome so that the old rocks of the Ordovician and Silurian periods again stood high in the centre of Cumbria. Rivers running down from the lofty centre of the dome began to cut a radial system of valleys into this dome, whose centre lay roughly at Scafell Pike.

This raising of high mountains in Alpine times meant that they provided an exposed and elevated region for the growth of glaciers as temperatures fell and the Ice Ages began some six hundred thousand years ago. There were probably three separate ice ages here, divided from one another by warmer periods, the whole era spanning the period from about six hundred thousand years ago to about ten thousand years ago. The last main glaciation, now termed the 'Devensian' by geologists, seems to have lasted from perhaps seventy thousand until fifteen thousand years ago and since then minor changes in

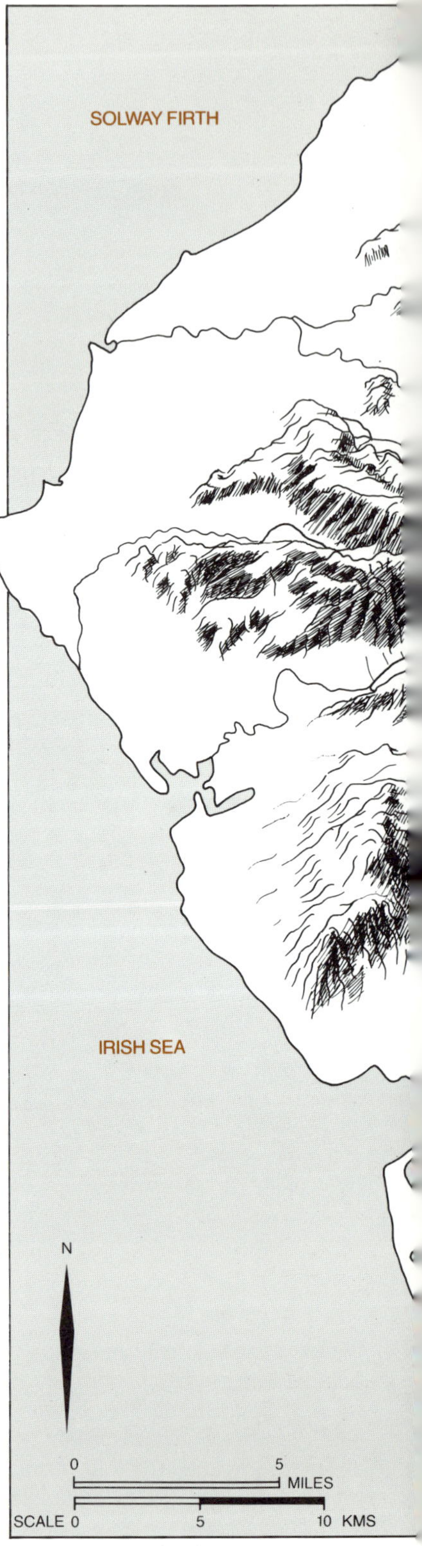

Cumbria from the south. The Pennines in the south and east and the coastal plains of the Solway Firth, Irish Sea and Morecambe Bay surround the remnants of the once much more massive mountains which now form the Lake District proper, with its highest points of Scafell, Helvellyn and Skiddaw.

temperature have given rise to small glaciers on the high fells up to as recently as ten thousand years ago.

The glaciers have had the major effect of widening and deepening the river valleys that had been cut into the Lake District dome. Ice has the capacity, when loaded with abrasive rock débris, to scour out basins in solid rock. These basins provided the hollows in the high mountains that are now occupied by the tarns and the bigger basins in the main valleys that are occupied by the lakes; so the lakes of Lakeland are really a legacy of glaciation. Blea Water, south-west of Haweswater, is the deepest Lake District tarn and Wast Water is the deepest lake. Frost acting on the high peaks and the valley sides supplied a mass of broken rock that the glaciers then used to scour out the valleys. Langdale and Borrowdale are classic examples of severely glaciated valleys with steep sides, the lakes and former lake beds of which are now filled in by post-glacial deposits. The delta of river sediments built into the head of Derwent Water by the River Derwent is rapidly reducing the size of the lake. The River Greta, flowing through Keswick, and Newlands Beck, coming off the Derwent Fells, poured massive quantities of sediment into a former vast lake, and now Derwent Water and Bassenthwaite Lake are the fragmented portions of that lake.

Outside the Lake District proper the glaciers had rather different effects. As the temperature rose and the ice melted in the lowlands, masses of rock débris removed by the glaciers from the mountains were dropped as 'ground moraine', 'boulder clay' or 'till' to form hummocky irregular ground, often with small badly drained hollows occupied by tarns.

When glaciers stopped advancing and had a period of stability, the ice-borne burden of rock débris would pile up at the snout of the glacier to form an 'end' or 'terminal' moraine. Both Windermere

Above: Wast Water, the deepest lake in the Lake District, lies in a deep rock basin gouged out by glaciers during the Ice Ages.
Below: In Langdale a lake has already been filled in by fast-flowing rivers. Frost-shattered scree is accumulating at the bottom of the glaciated valley sides.

Below: Sty Head Tarn looking north. Tarns or small lakes lie in ice-scoured hollows at the head of the glaciated valleys. Sty Head Tarn lies at the head of the western of the two main tributary valleys that unite to form Borrowdale. The upper end of the tarn has already been filled in by the streams coming off High Kern Knott and Great Slack.

and Coniston Water are partially dammed by such features.

Once the ice melted, the lake and tarn basins began to fill up with the sediments being carried down from the mountains by the streams flowing into them. The pollen produced by the plants growing near these stretches of water produces a 'rain' that falls into the water and is trapped in the sediments; in the saturated conditions it does not then decay. Each botanical species has unique pollen forms, and painstaking work by scientists such as Winifred Pennington has made it possible to calculate the relative balance of the plant communities since the end of the Ice Ages. The record of the growth of the forests after the glaciers melted and of their later clearance by man has been traced by this technique of pollen analysis.

On the gentler slopes of the higher hills, under conditions of high rainfall and poor drainage, peat has accumulated. Pollen grains also survive in the peat. Up to about 2000 ft (600 m), the remains of pine and birch trees can clearly be seen lying at the base of the peat, and it is thought that these woodland relics are evidence of a change of climate from drier to wetter conditions during the Bronze Age, beginning about 1200 BC and continuing into the Iron Age. Because organic matter survives in peat, it provides an important link between the geological and the archaeological dating evidence in the story of Cumbria. Charcoal left from the fires of Neolithic and Bronze Age man has survived in the peat together with the stone tools of these peoples. New techniques of radio-carbon dating have allowed scientists to date charcoal from peat found near the Langdale axe factory to about 2700–2500 BC. As new techniques are developed, no doubt an increasingly accurate time-scale of Cumbrian geology and early archaeology will be possible.

The Lake District proper – the high dome of ancient rocks that has already been described – stands proud of its fringes when viewed from every approach. To the visitor arriving via the M6 and A591 the southern fells, especially the Langdale Pikes, stand up strikingly when seen from the Staveley – Windermere road. From Carlisle the north-eastern fells, especially Carrock Fell, dominate the view and Skiddaw, an isolated mass, stands high above the northern approaches to Keswick.

In looking across these peaks it is important to bear in mind that the Lake District is divided into three geological zones: the smooth steep slopes of the Skiddaw Slates in the north; the rough, rugged, dramatic Borrowdale Volcanic rocks of the high central fells, and the lower rather flatter southern fells formed on the Silurian rocks. From the two major through routes across the Lake District, via Dunmail Raise (A591) and the Kirkstone Pass (A592), the changes can be seen very clearly. The Kirkstone Pass route is the more dramatic of the two, but it is a less easy road. The highest fells in the Borrowdale Volcanics are best approached up Langdale, Borrowdale or via Wasdale and the Duddon Valley from the west coast. The high wall of the Pennines forms a real barrier east of the Eden Valley. The A686 from Penrith to Alston provides splendid views westwards and the steepness of the road emphasizes the wall-like edge of the 'Alston block' section of the Pennines. The Stainmore Gap, followed by the A66, is the only other route through this high western edge of the Pennines. Cross Fell and Mickle Fell are lofty, tabular mountains of Carboniferous rocks that form the most distinctive summits on this edge, which is one of the major fault lines of England.

The Eden Valley is on the 'downthrow' side of the Pennine fault and the River Eden occupies this structural trough. The New Red Sandstones of this lower, more sheltered area produce red soils and have more arable crops growing on

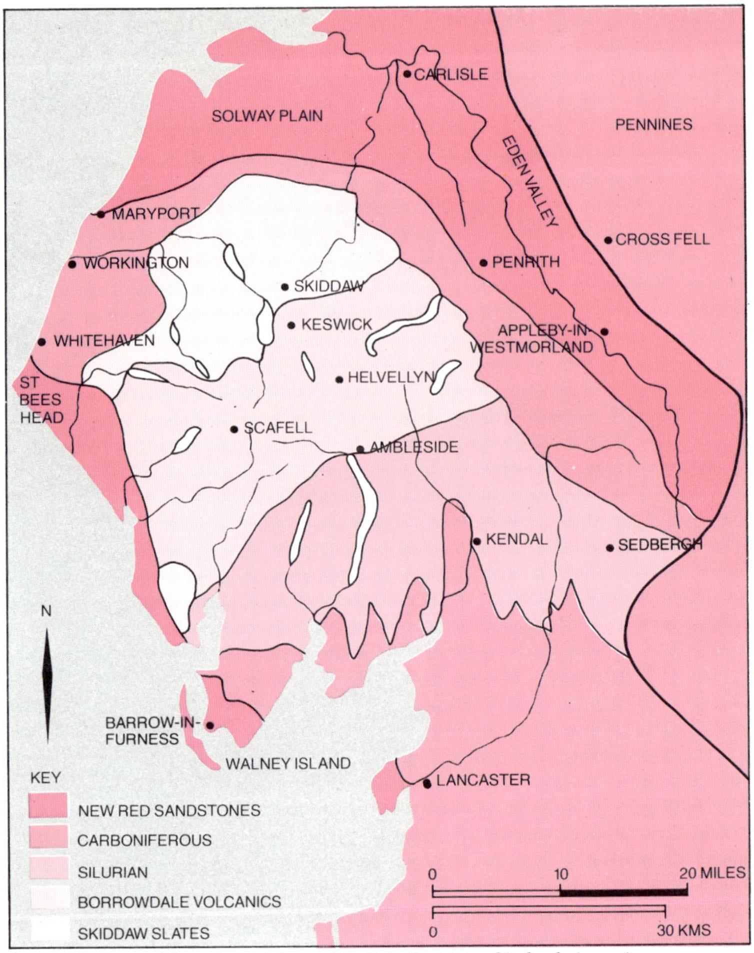

A generalized map of the major rock types of the Lake District and its bordering regions.

The Scafell range lies at the centre of the highest Lake District fells. The volcanic rocks of the Borrowdale Volcanic Series, criss-crossed by faults and mineral veins, have weathered into a variety of shapes under the attacks of rain and frost.

them than other parts of Cumbria can usually support. The major effect of the Ice Ages in the Eden Valley was to lay down ice-smoothed moraine of clay and boulders known as 'drumlins'. These give a hummocky surface to the vale through which the Eden twists its way northwards to Carlisle and produces what is graphically described as 'basket of eggs' topography. The Romans and the railway and motorway engineers have all exploited this natural routeway and thus Appleby, Penrith and Carlisle occupied key defensive sites in times of war and still occupy key market sites today.

The north and west fringes of Cumbria are zones of coastal lowland and in the main also areas of New Red Sandstone. But Carboniferous rocks surface in a virtually continuous arc closer to the Lake District proper. The oldest Carboniferous rocks are limestones, but above them coal-rich beds were formed which are known as the Coal Measures. These gave rise to a small but once important coalfield along the coast between Maryport and Whitehaven which in turn supported the three seaports of Maryport, Workington and Whitehaven and the steelworks at Workington.

The high fells of the western valleys of the Lake District almost reach the sea, but Low Furness (Furness is a Norse word meaning 'the far headland') is a distinctive area of limestone country. The limestone was penetrated by rich veins of high-quality haematite iron ore. This iron was worked from at least Norman times until the 1950s and towns such as Millon, Askam and Barrow owe their present character almost entirely to their nineteenth-century iron-making days.

The southern fringe of Cumbria, a continuation of Low Furness, is a mixture of limestone crags, patches of New Red Sandstones and wide tidal estuaries. It is more sheltered and milder than the higher areas; snow rarely lies long at Grange-over-Sands. The great Cistercian Abbey at Furness and the Augustinian Priory at Cartmel occupied sheltered sites amongst their farmlands. The estuaries of the Crake and Leven at Greenodd and that of the Kent between Grange and Arnside bring tidal flats and seabirds well inland. Greenodd is an attractive spot that was once a small port for the Southern Lake District. The summits of the limestone scars west of Kendal and north of Grange provide panoramic viewpoints of the southern fells of the Lake District.

The Lune Valley forms the south-eastern edge of Cumbria. Kirkby Lonsdale, Sedbergh, Dentdale and the Howgill Fells all now lie in administrative Cumbria. The Lune rises on the back (northern) slopes of the Howgill Fells and then flows through a dramatic gorge south of Tebay. Here road and rail are both channelled by this one route across the major east-west watershed of the Cumbrian-Pennine hills before climbing to Shap summit. The Lune Valley opens out southwards towards Kirkby Lonsdale, and finally the river reaches the sea at Lancaster. It is a beautiful valley and well worth exploring via the A683. High plateaux of limestone and Silurian Slates lie between the Lune and the Kent Valleys and from them many fine views of the Lakes and Morecambe Bay may be seen.

The Howgill Fells north of Sedbergh form a distinctive hill mass which stands up sharply from the surrounding valleys and offers some high-quality hill-walking – Cautley Spout and the Calf being the most popular spots as well as offering panoramic viewpoints.

The rocks mentioned have a marked impact on the appearance of different areas of Cumbria both in terms of natural and man-made features, so that geology is widely displayed in the works of man. In Kendal, Ulverston and Barrow the blocky, grey/white limestone is used for basic building construction. However, it is not a stone that lends itself to subtle carving and windowheads; sills and door jambs are often carved from the more amenable New Red Sandstone or Carboniferous Sandstone so that mouldings and dates can be worked in the softer rock. The New Red Sandstone was often carried some distance for such work: for example, Hawkshead Courthouse (now owned by the National Trust) has its window mullions and frames in sandstone in

Stone cottage in Watendlath. From the late seventeenth century slate has been the major building material in the region, and the National Park authorities insist on its being used wherever possible, at least for facing buildings.

an otherwise slate building. The slates of the southern and northern Lake District are used in the miles of dark stone walls and in the farm houses and in their hay and wool barns. Heavy blocks are used in walls and fine slates from Honister, Tilberthwaite or Elterwater are used for roofing. The Borrowdale Volcanics have some fine-grained ash slates in them but also many much more massive beds as well: huge blocks are often used as the quoinstones for houses and barns. In Eskdale by Devoke Water, in Ennerdale and on Shap Fell several varieties of granite provide beautiful stones. Shap granite, with its huge pink felspar crystals, is unique and makes a fine ornamental polished stone which has been used throughout England.

Many valuable mineral ores have been injected into the older rocks during several periods of volcanic activity and these have led to mines being developed, such as the copper mines around Coniston.

Climate and the Cumbrian Landscape

As well as the rocks, it is important to consider the influence of climate in producing the great variety of elements which make the present-day Cumbrian landscape. Rainfall increases with height and the temperature falls; soils are thinner on the higher slopes, and on the high fells everything combines to discourage lush plant growth and in turn human activity. Rainfall at Seathwaite in Borrowdale is recorded as being 120 in (3048 mm) per annum – the highest in England – and it is probably even more on the highest fells. Frost is recorded on more than a hundred nights a year, and plant cover on the exposed fells has to be an arctic or sub-arctic type – mosses, lichens, dwarf varieties of ling and willow, club mosses, some bilberry and crowberry, mountain sedge and bents.

Under natural conditions in Cumbria, woodland would probably

The high peaks, such as Great Gable with its summit in cloud, cause the air that rises over them to cool. This leads to clouds forming and, as it thickens, rain falls. The high peaks of the Lake District are the wettest and coldest places in England.

reach as high as 2000 ft (600 m) in the more sheltered areas but the effect of grazing by sheep and perhaps, also, by red deer in some areas of the eastern fells is to prevent regeneration of trees, with the result that poor-quality grazings of matgrass tend to dominate wide stretches of the upper slopes and ridges. Woodland survives only when protecting walls are carefully maintained or in areas such as screes and gullies where trees can establish themselves before sheep can get at them.

Oak, ash and alder are the most common woodland trees, although in some areas yew may grow well on middle slopes, as for example in Easedale near Grasmere and on the Furness fells above Coniston Water, while there are some famous ancient specimens in Borrowdale.

In badly drained hollows, marsh plants grow and an acid peat bog forms with heather, ling, bilberry, cotton grass and many species of rush and sedge. These areas of peat formation were once very important as sources for fuel. For example, the broad plateau between Kentmere and Longsleddale around Skeggleswater was a major peat-cutting area. On the lower slopes man has heavily modified the natural vegetation by cutting, burning, draining and liming the pastures and meadows. Better stock-grazing grasses such as bents and fescues became dominant and cattle can get good summer grazing from them. Bracken tends to spread fast if not carefully controlled and this can be seen well at Elterwater Common in Langdale where it has almost reached the top of the ridge between Langdale and Easedale.

The valley bottoms, if not occupied by a lake, offer good if often rather wet grazing for cattle. If they are very wet then alder woodland flourishes. Alder was a most useful tree, supplying wood for building, for fuel, and for charcoal-making for the gunpowder industry which was locally very important in the nineteenth century.

The natural vegetation of Cumbria is deciduous forest up to about 2000 ft (600m) above sea level. Here in Borrowdale, the yew survives from the ancient woodland.

PREHISTORIC AND ROMAN TIMES

The story of man in the Lake District is a long one, even though there is little evidence of an Old Stone Age or Paleolithic population. The Ice Ages of the Quaternary period lasted from around 600,000 to about 12,000 years ago. When the ice had retreated from the ice-scoured basins that became lakes and tarns, and plants and animals colonized the smoothed rock or glacial débris-covered surfaces, Mesolithic or Middle Stone Age man moved into the region.

Human communities were already well-established in the warmer region of southern England. Mesolithic peoples were hunters, fishers and gatherers of roots, berries and edible plants. They probably entered Britain across the lost land bridge that joined the south-east to the continent and which had not yet been eroded by the waters of the rising post-glacial seas. Their most typical sites were on river terraces and lake shores, where they could catch fish and hunt for birds. They shaped myriads of small stone flakes or 'microliths' to edge their tools and weapons and made larger scrapers, picks, awls, arrowheads and spearheads, and such objects provide the most frequent evidence of their temporary hunting sites. They also used bone for tools and harpoons and they probably wove a variety of basket-ware containers. They were not cultivators of crops though they may have kept semi-domesticated deer. These people seem only to have settled the western edge of Cumbria and their flint tools have been found on Walney Island and at Eskmeals, Drigg, and near St Bees Head.

It was perhaps around eight or nine thousand years ago that Britain became separated from the mainland of Europe. Around 5000 BC new groups of technically more advanced settlers reached the British Isles, probably sharing their new ideas with the natives. They have been termed the Neolithic or New Stone Age peoples. They were farmers, growing cereal crops and rearing animals; they occupied more permanent sites and therefore some evidence of their buildings, field systems and burial sites has survived. In Cumbria their earliest sites have been dated at about 4000 BC. These settlers had a major influence on the landscape. Their stone axes were very effective tools for clearing the ancient woodland. The plant pollen that accumulated in peats in this period has been examined in great detail during the last thirty years and it shows that trees were being felled and replaced by crops, weeds and grassland around 4000 BC, and that the elm in particular had declined severely by about 3000 BC. This decline is attributed to increased animal rearing, with the probable use of elm leaves for fodder. Work on the sediments laid down in lakes gives a similar picture and Dr Pennington has shown that the rate of accumulation of sediments in Devoke Water increased in early prehistoric times and accelerated around 1000 BC, suggesting that forest clearance and cultivation were leading to an increase in the rate at which soil was eroded from the banks and exposed hillsides and washed into the lakes. The field evidence on the granite uplands north of Devoke Water supports this picture because there are scores of clearance mounds, suggesting agricultural cultivation, and land clearance for many burial mounds of stones, implying a considerable agricultural population.

Ehenside Tarn is perhaps the most interesting Neolithic site in Cumbria and some of the finds from it are in Carlisle Museum. Some of the pottery found on this site probably came from Grimston in Yorkshire, and certain pieces resemble types made around Peterborough. Long stone axes of the Cumbrian type were found, one still with its wooden handle. Other wooden objects had survived in the peat and a dug-out canoe was also found. The wooden objects have widely ranging radio-carbon dates, from 3014–1570 BC, with the later finds belonging to the Bronze Age.

The Mesolithic tools and many of the Neolithic axes were found to have been made from a fine-grained greenish-grey volcanic tuff of the Borrowdale Volcanic Series. In 1947 the site from which some of the Cumbrian axes came was discovered on the screes just below Pike o' Stickle. Since then many more sites have been discovered on the high central fells where waste flakes, rough-outs and rejects can be found, and a cluster of axe factories lay around Scafell Pike. Below Pike o' Stickle, a working face on the tuffs shows where Neolithic and later Bronze Age workers broke off masses of the valuable rock prior to shaping it into rough-outs, some of which were sent to the coast for polishing.

The tuff has similar qualities to flint in that when struck, sharp flakes, themselves usable as blades, split off and a solid core is left

Right and below: Pike o'Stickle. This dramatic remnant of a volcanic mass had a valuable bed of volcanic tuff on its upper crags which provided Neolithic and early Bronze Age peoples with an important supply of stone for their tools. The area of their axe factory is detailed at right.

Mayburgh Henge, near Penrith. A single surviving standing stone is set within a high cobble bank.

The henge monument known as King Arthur's Round Table, near Eamont Bridge, one mile south of Penrith and a quarter of a mile from Mayburgh.

which can then be polished and sharpened as an axe. These Cumbrian axes have been traced all over Great Britain, showing that considerable Neolithic trade routes existed and that Lakeland axes were mainly made for export. Radio-carbon dating of charcoal from one of these sites gave dates of 2730 – 2550 BC. Within our area the bulk of the axe finds has come from the coastal plain and from the Eden Valley, but scattered finds have also come from within the Lake District proper. It is possible that the axes were moved to southern markets by sea routes; they were certainly important trade goods and were widely dispersed.

The First Monuments

The most significant form of monument left by the Neolithic and Bronze Age peoples is the henge, a form of ritual monument that gave way to the stone circle. Henge monuments consist of almost circular earthworks with one or more entrances, enclosing an area perhaps 100 yards across, though the sizes vary greatly. Mayburgh at Eamont Bridge, immediately south of Penrith, is the outstanding Cumbrian example. It now has one huge standing stone, or monolith, inside the high earth and pebble bank, though several more were standing in the eighteenth century when William Stukeley, the antiquary, visited it. Mayburgh is a Neolithic henge, perhaps dating from about 3000 BC. Near Mayburgh is a second henge known as King Arthur's Round Table, one of England's best henges, but less imposing than its neighbour. While the function of these monuments is still far from clear, it is reasonable to view them as temples whose banks and ditches define the sacred area within.

The Bronze Age culture seems to have reached the region in the third millennium BC. Its people built cairns, some of them surrounded by outer circles of stones which are smaller than the stones used in the ceremonial circles. At Gunnerkeld, on Shap Fells just to the east of the M6, there is an example of a cairn with two stone circles surrounding it. At Great Mell Fell, a National Trust property just to the north of Ullswater, there is a ditch around a burial mound. Elsewhere, collections of stone cairns survive which have been termed cairnfields: a good example is at Barnscar near Muncaster and another covers the granite plateau near Devoke Water. It is not certain whether such fields are concentrations of burial mounds or whether they represent stones piled up as the very early field systems were cleared of débris. Only excavation of more examples will reveal the truth, though several fields probably have examples of each.

The most striking monuments of all are the ceremonial stone circles. They are evocative, fascinating sites and they are still a mystery as far as their precise ritual function is concerned. Castlerigg, or Keswick Carles, a National Trust site a mile and a half east of Keswick, lies in a beautiful position with a 360-degree view from it. The 38 huge stones stand in a brooding circle and within the circle is a rectangular setting of ten stones whose date and function remain unexplained.

Swinside, near Millom on the west coast at the mouth of the Duddon Valley, is another such site, perhaps the most perfect example in the region. Like Castlerigg, the circle of standing stones has a diameter of about 150ft (45m) and the 55 surviving stones are bedded in a layer of rammed pebbles. Shap Stones has an avenue of stones leading to the stone circle which is damaged by the railway. Long Meg and her Daughters, near Little Salkeld, six miles north-east of Penrith, is in some ways the most dramatic of all these sites. Long Meg herself is a high detached standing stone, covered with 'cup and ring marks' of concentric circles and other patterns. She stands outside the main stone circle formed by her 'daughters'; they consist of 65 stones, mostly fallen, from an original total of about 70.

The surviving artefacts of the Bronze Age are few and far between in Cumbria. In those cairns that have proved to be burial cairns, simply decorated 'collared urns' have been found, and numbers of distinctive Bronze Age tools such as axes, spearheads, daggers and rapiers have come to light, especially in Furness and the Eden and Lune Valleys.

The Bronze Age may have lingered longer in the remote fastnesses of the Lake District. In England generally, the Iron Age arrived around 650 BC, but Clare Fell, one of Cumbria's best known archaeologists, concluded that the

Above: Long Meg and her Daughters, near Little Salkeld, is one of the best-preserved stone circles. Long Meg is of New Red Sandstone and heavily carved.
Below: Castlerigg Stone Circle, also known as Keswick Carles, was built c.2000 BC one mile east of Keswick. This view looks south to the Vale of St John and the Helvellyn range.
Bottom: Swinside stone circle, two miles west of Broughton-in-Furness, is seen with the dark mass of Thwaites Fell to the north-west.

Below: Carrock Fell, a dramatically sited walled hill fort covering five acres. It was built on the highest point in the north-east corner of the Lake District with the lowland of the Eden Valley below and the Pennine Wall to the east.
Bottom: Castle Crag hill fort, possibly a stronghold of the Brigantes. It stands high above Borrowdale almost due west of the Bowder Stone.

pre-Roman Iron Age still holds its secrets as far as the Lake Counties are concerned. Few Iron Age artefacts have so far been found in Cumbria. Outstanding was the Embleton Sword and its sheath found near Wythop Mill in the nineteenth century and now in the British Museum.

The major Iron Age features that can still be seen are the hill forts. Some of these, such as the one at Butts Beck Quarry near Dalton-in-Furness, may turn out to be Bronze Age rather than Iron Age in origin, as several in southern England are now known to be. They occupy marvellous sites, all of which must have been very difficult places to capture. The fort on Carrock Fell is an impressive ruin with stretches of its stone rampart still intact. Its walls encircle the summit of the very steep-sided fell of gabbro rock. Castle Crag fort, on the west shores of Haweswater below Birks Crag, is beautifully sited and has rock-cut ditches. Other fortified sites are Croglam Castle near Kirkby Stephen, Castlesteads above Natlands south of Kendal, and another Castle Crag in Borrowdale with a girdle of rubble ramparts and fine views over Derwent Water. It is thought that they were sites used by the British tribesmen of the Brigantes federation, and they reflect the fractious nature of the indigenous British societies.

The other visible Iron Age features are either just pre-Roman or Romano-British in date. These are the systems of stone banks and earthworks that are the surviving evidence of small settlements and individual farmsteads. The best-known example is at Ewe Close, about two miles south-west of Crosby Ravensworth village and east of the M6. A system of stone-built hut circles and a network of stone paddock walls survive in the middle of which there are the particularly well-preserved foundations of a large stone hut. The line of a Roman road can be traced nearby. The area at the head of the valley of the Lyvennet

Hadrian's Wall at Peel Crag. The faced wall stands high on the natural volcanic dike of the Whin Sill.

Roman milestone at Middleton, near Sedbergh, on the road from Ribchester to Carlisle.

The line of the Roman road that follows the High Street ridge. This road ran from Ambleside to Brougham.

Beck has several settlements scattered over it, usually single farmsteads which lie along the arc of limestone soils that forms Crosby Ravensworth, Orton and Crosby Garret Fells.

Roman Routes and Settlements

The Romans arrived in Great Britain as invaders and occupiers in AD 43 under the leadership of Emperor Claudius. It took them time to consolidate their conquest, but by AD 78 Julius Agricola had established Roman control as far north as the Forth-Clyde line in what is now Scotland. In order to control the Picts in Scotland the Romans needed an efficient system of good roads along which they could move troops quickly to meet any threat. The major route from Chester crossed the Ribble Valley at Ribchester, cut across the Forest of Bowland and followed up the east bank of the River Lune as far as Tebay. It then ran on to Brougham (Roman *Brocavum)* where it crossed the River Eamont and then made for Carlisle *(Luguvalium).*

This main south-north road was linked with the main road up the eastern side of England (Ermine Street) by a road called Stanegate which ran from Carlisle to Corbridge and by a second route using the Stainmore Gap. This route, followed now by the A66, was controlled by forts at Brough *(Verteris)* and Catterick *(Cateractonium).*

In AD 122, on the instructions of the Roman Emperor Hadrian, the wall bearing his name was built from Wallsend on the east coast as far as Bowness-on-Solway. A system of forts, and fortlets at one-mile intervals, continued this line westwards down the coast of the Irish Sea as far south as St Bees Head. The wall became the frontier with the Picts and, to its south, in Cumbria, a Romano-British society evolved.

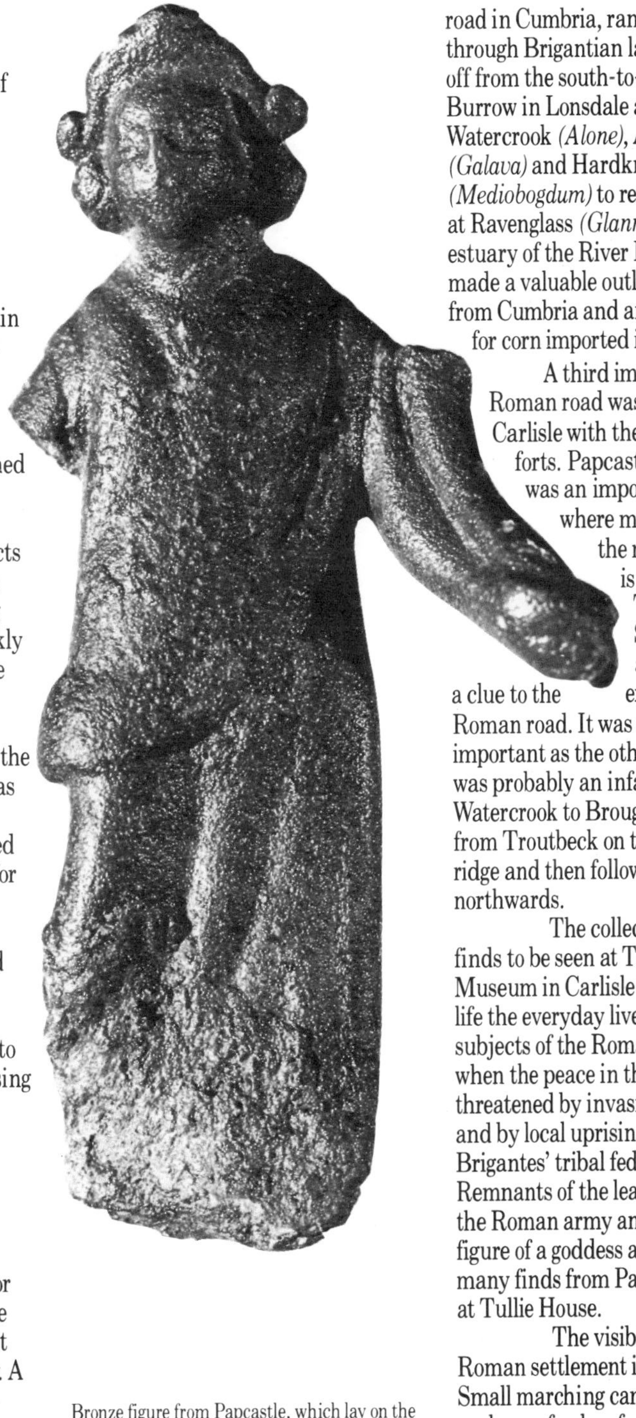

Bronze figure from Papcastle, which lay on the Roman road to the coast from Carlisle.

Another Roman route cut through the territory of the Brigantes, who were initially hostile to Roman rule but who, by the third century AD, seem to have been less so. This, the second most important Roman road in Cumbria, ran westwards through Brigantian lands, branching off from the south-to-north road at Burrow in Lonsdale and going via Watercrook *(Alone)*, Ambleside *(Galava)* and Hardknott *(Mediobogdum)* to reach the Irish Sea at Ravenglass *(Glannaventa)* on the estuary of the River Esk. This road made a valuable outlet for metals from Cumbria and an inward route for corn imported into the region.

A third important length of Roman road was that built to link Carlisle with the chain of coastal forts. Papcastle *(Derventio)* was an important route centre where minor roads joined the main road which is now the A595. The name 'High Street', suggesting a paved road, gives a clue to the existence of another Roman road. It was never as important as the other three and it was probably an infantry route from Watercrook to Brougham, climbing from Troutbeck on to the High Street ridge and then following that ridge northwards.

The collections of Roman finds to be seen at Tullie House Museum in Carlisle help to bring to life the everyday lives of the far-flung subjects of the Roman Empire in days when the peace in the North was threatened by invasions by the Picts and by local uprisings of tribes in the Brigantes' tribal federation. Remnants of the leather tents used by the Roman army and a draped bronze figure of a goddess are amongst the many finds from Papcastle to be seen at Tullie House.

The visible evidence of the Roman settlement is very varied. Small marching camps, remnants perhaps of only a few nights' occupation, may survive as very low earthworks in rush-covered fields, as at Troutbeck near Field Head. The south-west corner of this camp is clipped by the A66. From this site the native hill fort on Carrock Fell could easily be watched. At Ravenglass, a single stone building, the bath house, is all that can be seen of the fort, which is now known as Walls Castle and was built to guard the harbour and port.

At Ambleside, an excavation by R. G. Collingwood between 1913 and 1920 produced an idea of the appearance of a Roman military fort. *Galava* (National Trust) was beautifully sited at the head of Windermere at Borrans Field, partly for defence but presumably also to make use of the lake for transport. As so often happened, a native settlement grew up outside the fort and this one had a leather-working industry. That it was attacked is clear because a tombstone found nearby records that Julius Romanus, a record clerk, was killed in the fort by the enemy. Pottery found there shows that *Galava* was inhabited until about 383.

At Carlisle, the impact of Rome was at its greatest. It is thought that a sub-group of the Brigantes, the Carvetii, may have had their capital at Carlisle and by 250 have gained 'Civitas' status, providing some

Above: Walls Castle, Ravenglass. These are the only standing remains of the Roman fort of *Glannaventa* which overlooked the estuaries of the Rivers Mite and Esk. The building was once the bathhouse – which must have been welcome to soldiers who had marched from Ambleside (*Galava*) via Hardknott (*Mediobogdum*) to the coast.

degree of self-government; if so, major civic buildings such as a forum and basilica would have existed. The Eden Valley is the most fertile part of Cumbria, so *Luguvalium* had food supplies nearby. The Roman settlement, lying on a high sandstone bluff on a promontory between the River Eden to the north and the Caldew and the Petteril to west and east, is superbly sited – as can be sensed when one stands on the battlements of the Norman castle and looks northwards. However, despite its excellent position, it is not clear how Hadrian's Wall was related to this important settlement. The major Roman military site was not at Carlisle but at Stanwix on the north side of the Eden.

The most dramatic of all Roman sites in Cumbria is that of Hardknott *(Mediobogdum)* in Upper Eskdale. This stone-walled fort guarded the route from Ambleside to Ravenglass and it was built on a high spur at just over 700ft (210m) which projects westwards between the Upper Esk Valley and Hardknott Gill, overlooking a valley site at Brotherilkeld that was later to be favoured as a farm site by the monks of Furness Abbey. Much of the exterior wall of the fort has survived or been restored and it is one of the most impressive man-made features of the central Lake District and very accessible to the more courageous of motorists. The fort has been much restored by the Department of the Environment, and the outer walls present an ashlar face of shaped stones to the visitor. Inside, the standard plan of a Roman fort can be recognized with surviving remains of the granary, the administration block and the commander's house. The bath house was situated outside the south-east gateway of the fort. On the flattened spur to the east of the fort was the parade ground which must have been a bleak spot during the long Cumbrian winters. Various finds of coins and pottery put a last date of habitation by the Romans at just about the end of the second century AD.

For the Roman or military enthusiast, Hadrian's Wall and the west coast forts provide foci for an entire holiday of exploration. Hadrian's Wall enters Cumbria at Birdoswold and follows the north side of the Irthing Valley as far as Stanwix; it crosses the River Eden at Carlisle and reaches Bowness-on-Solway. From Bowness it gives way to a series of coastal forts, which were almost certainly linked by a Roman road, as far south as Moresby. It is thought that Maryport *(Alauna)* was the major control point of this line of defence. The earthworks of this fort survive and a public footpath marks their southern edge.

North of the Wall, two important forts were built at Netherby and Bewcastle. Bewcastle is a classic example of a fine site. It was originally chosen by the Romans and in turn sheltered a Saxon Christian site, a Viking farm, a small Norman castle and a thirteenth-century church, but it did not expand beyond the Roman walls until the early thirteenth century. It is not clear whether these forts were built as outposts of the Wall or as garrison towns in an area of Brigantian territory that extended well to the north.

Above: Bewcastle – a fort 6 miles (10km) north of Hadrian's Wall. The medieval church, late thirteenth-century castle and the manor lie inside the earthworks of the Roman fort.
Far left and left: Hardknott Fort, built by the Romans to control the route from Ambleside to Ravenglass. It probably functioned between AD90 and 190. Remains of the granaries are in the foreground, the administration block behind. Also visible are the commander's house and the west angle turret, with Eskdale beyond.

AFTER THE ROMANS

In the last twenty years the picture of the Dark Ages has, to a great extent, been redrawn, or, more correctly, the details are being filled in more firmly than before. Archaeologists working at Carlisle have begun to piece together the sequence of events after the Romans left the town, and old sources such as Bede's *Ecclesiastical History of the English Nation,* written in the eighth century AD, can now be read in the context of new archaeological evidence. It is still true, however, that less is known about the period after the end of Roman rule around 410 than about the period from the ninth century up to the Norman conquest.

One reason for the lack of evidence in this period is almost certainly that there were very few people living in the upper valleys amongst the Lake District fells. The recent work of the Carlisle Archaeological Unit in its 1980 season has revealed the foundations of Saxon timber buildings on the site where the Marks and Spencer store has since been built. A silver pin, three ninth-century coins and a loomweight have also been found – at least enough to show that the Saxons were active there. Certainly, the view expressed by archaeologists such as Eric Birley, writing about Papcastle, and Mike McCarthy, writing about Carlisle, is that town life did not stop when the Romans left.

After their departure the essentially British/Celtic-speaking nature of the population re-established itself – if indeed the Romans had ever much altered the local cultures other than along the narrow zones fringing their major routes. The name 'Cumberland', which has been used as the basis for Cumbria, is derived from *Cymru,* meaning 'fellow countrymen'; it was used by the Britons to describe themselves and is now the Welsh word for 'Wales'. In 615 Aethelfrith, King of Northumbria, cut the Celtic North-West in two, severing Wales from the early Scottish 'Celtic' kingdom of Strathclyde which stretched from Galloway into Lancashire during the late sixth and seventh centuries.

Many place-names survive as reminders of the British phase of settlement in the north-west of England: for example, *pen,* as in Penrith and Penruddock, meaning 'head'; *blaen,* as in Blencathra, meaning 'point' or 'top', and most of the river names of the region such as Esk *(isca),* meaning 'water', and Derwent *(derva)* meaning 'oak'. The highest concentration of Celtic names occurs in the north-east corner of Cumberland, perhaps an area that was least attractive to later invaders. The modern Welsh *caer,* meaning 'fort', appears in Carrock Fell, probably in Carlisle, and in Cardew and Castle Carrock.

Anglo-Saxon inroads

The Anglo-Saxon settlers approached the region via the three natural routes – the Aire Gap from the south, the Tyne Gap from the north-east (both used later by railways), and the Stainmore (Brough) Gap from the east – all of which had been used by the Romans several hundred years before. Presumed early Saxon place-names with *ham* and *ing* elements, meaning respectively 'farm' or 'settlement' and a 'group of people', survive. For example, following the Aire Gap route we find Bentham, Tatham, Beetham, Heversham and Whicham, and many associated farmstead sites denoted by the *ton* place-name ending, which also means 'farm' or 'settlement'. From the north-east, perhaps following the line of the Roman road to the coastal forts, settlers moved in to found or to re-name Dearham and Brigham, with many more associated 'tons' appearing nearby. 'Inglewood' means the English wood and implies early English settlement via the Tyne Gap (the Forest of Inglewood was a major medieval element of the Cumbrian landscape). Place-names such as Skelton, Dalston and Orton are all Saxon. Skelton and Dalston are also relatively compact settlements with, round them, remnants of ancient field systems of a Saxon type. These villages are early, pre-Norman Conquest units in an area that was otherwise settled late.

The Danes established their settlements and influence over Northumbria by the third quarter of the ninth century and their presence was especially important in the Carlisle area and in the Vale of Eden.

Their most common place-name forms end in *by,* meaning 'farm' or 'village'; *thorpe,* a 'farm' or 'hamlet', and *thwaite,* a 'meadow'. As the Scandinavian influence was so strong in Cumbria, it is thought that the lingua-franca of the population at the time of the Norman conquest was still Old Norse and Old Danish, and that many Norse place-names were in fact not given to settlements until after the Conquest. A quick look at the map shows many 'thwaite' place-names immediately to the south of Carlisle. The map square 3040 has the following: Curthwaite, Thethwaite, Thwaite and Cockleythwaite. The 'by' names can be picked out west of Carlisle, for example at Thursby and then on the coast at Allonby. The area between the B5307 and the A596 from Carlisle west to the coast is spattered with 'by' place-name endings – Oughterby, Wiggonby, Thornby, etc.

The Scandinavian word for a church, *kjerk,* comes to our language as 'kirk' at Kirkhampton and Kirkbridge. Anyone who has visited Iceland or Norway will immediately sense similarities in the naming of natural features. If one starts a typical walk in Cumbria at the 'beck' (Old Norse *bekkr,* a 'stream') in the 'dale' (Old Norse *dalr,* a 'valley') and then climbs up on to the 'fell' *(fjoll),* perhaps past a 'fall' or 'force' *(foss),* one's progress is punctuated by Scandinavian names. On the hills there may be names ending in syllables such as 'scale(s)' *(skalar),* 'ergh' *(erg)* or 'sett' *(saetr),* all words describing the summer pasture and the temporary huts that settlers farming in the Scandinavian upland tradition established further up the valleys. Hawkshead and Ambleside are both derived from *saetr* endings.

Norse names replaced the Celtic settlement names in the Lake District core and there was virtually no intervening Anglo-Saxon phase of settlement, at least as recorded by place-name evidence in the Central Fells. How did this settlement of Scandinavians take place? Professor H. P. R. Finburg puts it in perspective when he says that 'they seem to have come as boatloads of wandering immigrants, among whom there was little or no military cohesion and who were content to occupy unwanted relatively unattractive lands'.

W. G. Collingwood, writing in 1925, produced a tidy model to show how a key village, to which a 'by' ending was given, was named after the group or folk leader. His followers or retainers may then have been allocated subsidiary holdings further up the valley when they built a homestead *(booth)* or meadow enclosure *(thwaite).* The valley head was then left to the wild boar, swine or *gris.* He quoted the Haweswater area to illustrate his thesis. Bornby is Bondeby, meaning a statesman's house; further up the valley is Thornthwaite – an outlying farm. Even higher up the valley is Whelter, its *ergh* ending meaning a shieling or summer hut. Archaeological work has shown this pattern to be true. Finally the uppermost stretch of the valley, in the days before it was flooded by Haweswater, was known as Swindale: the valley of the pigs. Thus Norse settlers colonized a Cumbrian valley which they settled in the same way that they would have used a valley in their homeland in Norway.

The Early Christians

Christianity had already reached Great Britain before the departure of the Roman armies and it has been assumed that Roman Britain in the early fifth century was Christian. Bishops already existed and Peter Salway in *Roman Britain* suggests that in 'the first half of the fifth century . . . it is not difficult to imagine bishops and clergy as clients of local "tyrants" and lesser notables throughout the old provinces; after the collapse of order in the middle of the century some crossed to Gaul, others may well have retreated gradually westward'.

An important early Christian influence was that of the monastic system, which evolved in the fifth century in Ireland, whence missionaries set out for the Cumbrian coast. The earliest surviving church building in Cumbria is the west tower at Morland, which is unquestionably pre-Conquest; earlier churches were probably built of wood and could not survive. The remains of the Celtic Christian phase and of the later Viking Christian phases are to be found in the crosses and the 'hogback' tombstones that survive in some Cumbrian churchyards. Professor Nikolaus Pevsner paid the famous Bewcastle Cross the compliment of

Irton Cross, a Saxon cross dating from the ninth century.

Gosforth Cross – a tenth-century shaft with a wheel head covered in Anglo-Viking carving.

One of two hogback tombs from Gosforth Church; these are Anglo-Saxon in style.

saying that 'the crosses of Bewcastle and of Ruthwell in Dumfriesshire . . . are the greatest achievement of their date in the whole of Europe, their date being the late seventh century'. The imagery used in the Bewcastle Cross perhaps came from Coptic (Egyptian, early Christian) monasticism; this monastic influence reached Cumbria via southern France, Ireland and south-west Scotland. The handling of the birds and beasts in the scrolls on the Bewcastle Cross is outstanding. A further twenty-one early crosses survive in west Cumberland.

By the late ninth century Viking influences replaced the early Saxon traditions and a later generation of crosses was produced. The most famous of these is at Gosforth. With its distinctive wheel head it stands nearly fifteen feet tall in Gosforth's churchyard and is of the Danish Jellinge style. Inside Gosforth church are two hogback tombstones. Others are to be seen at Appleby St Michael, Aspatria, Crosscanonby, Kirkby Stephen, Lowther, Penrith and Plumbland.

THE NORMAN PERIOD

Modern Cumbria was formed in 1974 from a union of the two counties of Cumberland and Westmorland to which was added the northern part of Lancashire known as Furness and Cartmel. In addition, the north-western corner of the old West Riding of Yorkshire, focussing on Sedbergh, was also absorbed.

Domesday Book, drawn up in 1086 at the command of King William I, has no separate entries for the area. The few scattered entries that do exist come under the Yorkshire section. This reflects the very fluid and complex border politics of the late eleventh century. In 945 King Dunmail was King of Cumbria and vassal to the English King Edmund. Following an unsuccessful rebellion against Edmund, his lands were given to King Malcolm I of Scotland, and Cumbria thus became a fief of the Crown of England, but not a fief held within the Kingdom of England (a somewhat confusing statement to modern ears). Finally, in 1092, William II (Rufus) established the present boundary between Scotland and England and took the 'land of Carlisle' into his kingdom. He confirmed his authority in this area by building a series of castles.

Origins of the Counties

William II made grants of land in what is now Cumbria to a number of powerful nobles and at the start of Henry I's reign the Appleby area was termed the Barony of Appleby, Applebyshire or Westmorland. The Barony of Kendal was also recognized as a separate feudal holding. The problem of controlling powerful nobles led Henry I to establish two Sheriffs as his own direct representatives, one to control the County of Carlisle and another for Westmorland, which consisted of the Baronies of Kendal and Appleby.

Cumberland, first mentioned as a county in 1178, was more complex in its origins than Westmorland. Separate baronies, that is, large feudal lordships, existed for Gilsland, in the north-east; Allerdale; Copeland (later Egremont) and Cockermouth which formed a group down the west coast, and the Barony of Greystoke which lay in the south-east of Cumberland. Carlisle and the area to the south of it remained in Royal hands as the Forest of Inglewood. Allerdale was also referred to in 1192 as a forest. The merging and dividing of inheritances is a very complex story but Cumberland remained subdivided for administrative purposes into four 'wards', rather than the more common 'hundreds', until the nineteenth century: these were the Eskdale, Cumberland, Leath and Allerdale Wards. These ancient components of the area remained the bases of its organization until the Poor Law Unions, when the Census districts and finally the local government areas replaced them.

Norman Castles

Now the administrative structure of modern Cumbria began to appear. The most dramatic and interesting buildings of that period are, of course, the castles, abbeys and parish churches. The origins of many of the castles are interwoven with the stories of the market towns. In some instances the markets grew up under the protection of the castles; in others, the castles appear to have been located at key sites which had already become towns; several of these sites had been chosen earlier by the Romans, as happened at Carlisle.

The first group of castles includes those built by William II between 1087 and 1091. Brough, Appleby, Brougham, Penrith and Carlisle Castles were established, initially with earthen mottes, banks, ditches and timber palisades, to guard the Eden Valley route from Scotland. The west coast route was initially protected by castles built at Cockermouth and Egremont. Gradually stone replaced wood and splendid buildings of which only fragments survive, as at Penrith, were built. From them tributary baronies were administered, and in times of invasion they were required to serve as bastions against the Scots, not always successfully. In 1173, for instance, William the Lion of Scotland took Appleby and Brough, but failed to take Carlisle.

The history of Cumbria's castles is long and fascinating, and any visitor to the region could spend an entire holiday visiting nothing but castles. In this book we are limited to giving just a sample of the many sites and buildings, but hope that their characteristic flavour emerges.

Brougham Castle is superbly sited at a key strategic point already exploited by the Romans, who built *Brocavum* at the point where their Stainmore road crossed the

Above: Brough Castle, built by William II and restored in the seventeenth century by Lady Anne Clifford. It stands within the defences of the Roman fort of *Verteris* which was built to control the Stainmore Gap.
Below: Penrith Castle, built in 1397–99 by William Strickland who was later to become Bishop of Carlisle (1399–1419). Penrith is a compact courtyard castle; less of it now stands than when this view was painted. From Ackerman's *Picturesque Tour of the English Lakes* (1821).

Above and below: Brougham Castle. It was built c.1200 inside the defences of the Roman fort *Brocavum* and was also later restored by Lady Anne Clifford. Both the Roman and medieval forts guarded the important bridge-point of the River Eamont where the road from Stainmore crosses it to join the main north-south road at Penrith. The lower view is by P. de Wint.

River Eamont. The massive keep was built in stone in the late twelfth century and raised by one storey in the thirteenth. A deeply cut moat was topped by a stone screen wall in the fourteenth century and many buildings were gradually added inside the courtyards against the wall. A late thirteenth-century main gate was duplicated by an early fourteenth-century outer gate. In the reign of Stephen (1135 –54) the castle fell to the Scots, and after it was retaken in 1153 it was given to the Vipont family; later in the mid fourteenth century, it passed to the Cliffords. Lady Anne Clifford restored it and she died at Brougham in 1676. The Earls of Thanet let it decay and in 1714 it was stripped of its lead and timber.

Whereas Brougham Castle sits peacefully on the terrace above the River Eamont among trees and grazing cows, Egremont Castle has become the core of a busy market town and the traffic swirls round its outer bailey. Egremont is well sited on a crag set within a loop of the River Ehen which protects it to the north. The market town has grown up on the north side of the river. King William II built the original motte which forms the highest part of the site, but around 1130 – 40 William de Meschines built a stone castle slightly to the south of the motte. An impressive gateway and a stretch of screen wall with much herringbone masonry still survive, as well as a spread of foundations.

William de Meschines was Lord of the Barony of Copeland, a large territory which stretched from the River Duddon in the south to the River Derwent in the north and ran from the higher fells to the sea in the west. The later owners of the castle make a distinguished list – the Percys (Earls of Northumberland), the Seymours (Dukes of Somerset), and the Wyndhams, who held it in 1751 as Lords Egremont. An attractive triangular market place lies to the north of the castle on the north bank of the River Ehen. In 1794 the historian W. Hutchinson praised the 'Clean little Town . . . [in which] much of the Countenance of antiquity is retained'. Pevsner said, with some surprise: 'It is quite a handsome sight for an industrial Cumberland town.'

Above: Lady Anne Clifford (1590–1676) who died at Brougham. After two unhappy marriages she devoted herself to restoring her family's castles and to improving their estates.

Cockermouth Castle is notable partly because of its magnificent site but also because an enthusiast can read such a lot about it in J. Bernard Bradbury's excellent *History of Cockermouth*. Bradbury queries the William II dating for the castle and gives the first specific mention of the building as being in 1222, when William de Fortibus was Lord. It is built on a promontory at the confluence of the Rivers Cocker and Derwent. A spur of hard rock stands in the angle of the confluence and this triangular site accommodated a defended courtyard with a round tower facing west at the tip of the promontory. A moat and ditch were cut across its neck. These were later filled and the 'Percy Wing' built along it in the late fourteenth century. In 1400 the massive, and surviving, gatehouse was built and the courtyard, still in use, has had several phases of domestic buildings added, culminating in the offices built in 1904.

There are several other castle sites in the region, many of them open to the public. The distinctive pele towers of Cumbria will be discussed in the next chapter, as most of them are rather later than the castles and represent a lower level in the social hierarchy.

Egremont Castle. This well-sited twelfth-century fortress guarded the west-coast route and provided a base from which a powerful barony was administered.

The Monastic Impact

The second great achievement of the Normans was the building or rebuilding of parish churches and the founding of a number of important monasteries. As baronies, honours and manors were awarded to their followers by the Norman rulers, so the new lords either built or rebuilt the churches of their vills and manors. A surprisingly large number of early parish churches has survived.

The encouragement of the monastic orders under Norman patronage led to the foundation of many monasteries in areas where previously the Church had made relatively little influence. The Cistercian Order (founded in Cîteaux in France in 1098) particularly emphasized manual labour in isolated places. In 1127, at Furness, in the Vale of the Deadly Nightshade, a group of monks of the Order of Savigny settled and began to build their monastery. In 1147 this order was merged with the Cistercian Order and the building of the beautiful red sandstone buildings began, using stones hewn from quarries cut into the flanks of the narrow valley. A large proportion of the monastery, especially of the lay buildings, survives to give us a remarkable idea of the scale and importance of these great houses. (Furness was indeed second only to Fountains Abbey, the wealthiest Cistercian house at the time of the Dissolution in 1535.) Although much of the nave of the church has gone, a large part of the east end remains, as do parts of the cloister, an especially fine chapter house, the dormitory, the guest house, the kitchen and a good portion of the Abbot's house.

The monastic impact of Furness Abbey spread far beyond its buildings and can still be traced back into the fells of High Furness and beyond Cumbria. The Cistercians were given huge tracts of little-used land, including nearly all the part of old Lancashire known as Furness and a lot of land in Eskdale and in Borrowdale. They had two main sources of wealth: iron and wool. There was a relationship between the two activities because charcoal was essential for the smelting of the local iron ore, and, as hillsides were cleared of timber for charcoal burning, land became available for sheep and cattle rearing, and this grazing then prevented regeneration of the woodland.

The major estates of Furness Abbey lay between Windermere and Coniston Water and the area has a number of 'park' place-names as well as a number of others

Furness Abbey, near Barrow-in-Furness. The beautiful Norman doorways that led into the chapter house give a hint of what the great Cistercian abbey must have looked like before the Dissolution.

that give interesting clues to the past functions of those settlements. The park names refer to areas of enclosed ground and occur only after the Norman Conquest. Some, such as the adjoining High Dale Park, Middle Dale Park and Low Dale Park, relate to an original large deer park which dates from the Abbacy of Alexander Banks. In 1516 he set out a deer park which was subdivided later, presumably after the Dissolution, to form three farms.

Oxen Park and Stott (meaning 'young stock') Park would seem to have had very specific stock-rearing functions. Abbot Park, Lawson Park and Park-a-Moor were all probably sheep 'granges' or outfarms of the Abbey. These Furness estates lay a long way from the Abbey and so a major grange was built at Hawkshead at which a courthouse was established. This survives as an attractive slate building with red sandstone mullions and is now a National Trust property with exhibitions mounted by the Abbot Hall Museum, Kendal. Hawkshead itself bears the stamp of the post-Dissolution prosperity it secured under the patronage of the Sandys family, one of whom, as Archbishop of York, in 1585 founded the grammar school which Wordsworth was later to attend. The Archbishop also had Hawkshead established as a separate parish. Adam, another member of the family, secured a charter for a market and two fairs a year in the early seventeenth century. Hawkshead became an important wool market and its fairs were widely attended for the sale of sheep and cattle.

Hawkshead only secured its market after the Dissolution because Dalton-in-Furness was the market town directly under the patronage of the Abbey. A charter of 1239 granted it a fair and confirmed its market, and it flourished until 1535, but then quickly lost ground to Ulverston and Hawkshead. The lay power of the Abbot of Furness in Dalton seems to have been represented by the building of the 'castle' or, more accurately, the tower that stands in the long market place. It was probably built for his secular court and as a prison for debtors and other delinquents in the Abbot's jurisdiction.

Another side to ecclesiastical overlordship was experienced closer to the Abbey, when the village of Sellargrath, which probably lay near the west gate, was cleared away by Abbot Banks in order to create another large deer park, his 'New Park'. Park House still lies to the south of the Abbey, and Abbots Wood is to the north.

Furness Abbey – the choir and north transept. The abbey was built of New Red Sandstone cut from the sides of the valley in which it stands.

Shap Abbey. The sixteenth-century west tower is the chief surviving element of this small, isolated abbey which was founded in about 1191 by Premonstratensian canons (an order originating at Prémontré, near Laon, France).

Shap Abbey lies high on the eastern fells on the banks of the River Lowther on a site that must have been extremely bleak in winter. Like several monasteries, it moved from its original setting, which was at Preston near Kendal, transferring to the new site in about 1200. The earliest surviving work at the west end of the chancel is of the thirteenth century; the main survival is the tower, which must have been completed only just before the Dissolution.

Shap was quite well endowed, although not on the scale of Furness. The founder, Thomas Gospatric, granted the Abbey a considerable area of land near to it and also common rights at Raf(s) and in the surrounding area for 60 cows; for 20 mares to run in the woods; for

500 sheep with their young until the age of three; for five yoke of oxen, and also for wood for the Abbey, for timber, fire, hedging and other necessities. When the Abbey was dissolved in 1534 its estates went to the Wharton family who held them until the eighteenth century, when the Lowthers added them to their already large estates. As well as 44 tenements or dwellings at Shap, a further 22 were listed at 'Renegill' Grange, and if this was the modern Wren Gill at the head of Longsleddale it implies that a big loss of population must have taken place at some later date. Fourteen more tenements lay at 'Keild' (Keld) and 'Thornshappe' (Thornship) – certainly more dwellings than exist today.

A network of tracks spread out from the Abbey up into the isolated eastern valleys of Lakeland. In some cases, as at Thornthwaite, a surviving well-built packhorse bridge is a clue to a formerly important track which may have linked the Abbey with its Bampton estate, where the name 'Bampton Grange' survives.

At Cartmel there was a house of Augustinian canons. Their church, containing much Norman work, survived the Dissolution to become the present parish church. This makes it of great interest as a pre-Dissolution religious building with much of its original layout surviving. There is a fine Norman south door and the chancel has much Early English work. Inside, the mid fifteenth-century choir stalls with misericords survive as does the Harrington monument of 1347 which, says Pevsner, is 'sculpturally a monument of prime importance'. George Preston of Holker Hall carried out a big restoration in 1618 – 23, adding an interesting west screen and stall backs (by his work Preston may well have saved an important building). Of the other monastic buildings at Cartmel, only the gatehouse survives, forming part of the attractive market square and now owned by the National Trust.

Lanercost, like Cartmel an Augustinian house, also preserves the monastic church. Continual Scottish raids meant that the earliest buildings, founded in 1166 by Robert de Vaux, have not survived. The dominant theme is Early English work of the thirteenth century. As at Cartmel, very little of the monastic building remains apart from the west range which Sir Thomas Dacre turned into a house. Perhaps he chose to do this because of the lovely setting by the River Irthing. A defensive 'pele tower' remains at Lanercost, designed to protect the priors from Scottish raiders.

Parish Churches

The other principal contribution made by the Normans that is still visible in the landscape is their parish churches. Sixty Cumbrian churches contain some evidence of Norman work and 21 others have documentary evidence of Norman origins, although there is no surviving Norman work to be seen. As has been shown, the early settlements skirted the edge of the high fells, and the Norman parish churches, some of which almost certainly replaced late Saxon buildings, echo this settlement pattern.

Some settlements evolved round an early church and were renamed after the church was founded. Kirkbride and Bridekirk are both named after a church *(kjerk)* dedicated to St Bridget, sometimes known as St Bride, an Irish saint who died in about 523. This would suggest that they were sixth- or seventh-century foundations, although no buildings from this early date survive. Kirkoswald is dedicated to King Oswald of Northumbria who died in about 642, so is probably another ancient foundation, as are all churches dedicated to St Kentigern (St Mungo). Kirkbampton, Kirkby Lonsdale and Kirkby Stephen are all place-names incorporating the church element, and all contain Norman work. Architecturally, Kirkby Lonsdale is the most outstanding.

Three miles east of Carlisle is the church of St Leonard which has an almost perfect Norman apse with pilaster strips unlike anything seen in other Cumbrian churches. The north-west of the region has many Norman churches or, to be more accurate, churches with some Norman evidence in them; few were not much altered in later periods. Aspatria and Bromfield are both dedicated to St Kentigern, and Brigham is dedicated to St Bridget, reflecting the Irish Celtic influence in that area. Down the west coast Gosforth, as well as having its outstanding collection of hogback tombstones and its famous cross, has Norman work in it. Ulverston is a Norman church, and in the south-east corner of the region Kirkby Lonsdale is one of the finest and most complex of the region's Norman churches. Two churches that presumably superseded pre-Norman preaching crosses, Crosby Garrett and Crosby Ravensworth, have important Norman evidence and there are traces of similar work at Kirkby Stephen and Sedbergh.

Appleby's churches both have Norman work, and in the surrounding area is an important group of churches, at Kirkby Thore, Milburn, Long Marton and Morland, which all have post-Conquest evidence in them. The latter two also have almost certain traces of Saxon masonry. Near Ullswater, Dacre and Barton churches have Norman origins, though further north and east, probably because of the politically unsettled character of the area, there seem to be fewer Norman remains in the churches. Denton and Kirklinton are both Norman, and Kirkcambeck, if the dedication to St Kentigern is to be trusted, must originally have been an early foundation.

In the lowlands of Cumbria around the Lakeland core some eighty churches existed by around 1200, at which time the massive pillars, rounded arches and squat towers gave way to the pointed arches of the Early English style.

THE MEDIEVAL LANDSCAPE

The Normans made a profound mark on the region both administratively and architecturally. They created new lordships or baronies to establish a barrier zone of communities that were strongly motivated to protect themselves against the Scots. These new lords, loyal followers of William I and later Norman Kings, invariably built castles as their administrative and military centres, as at Egremont, and made gifts to the church, either by endowing monastic foundations or by building or adding to parish churches.

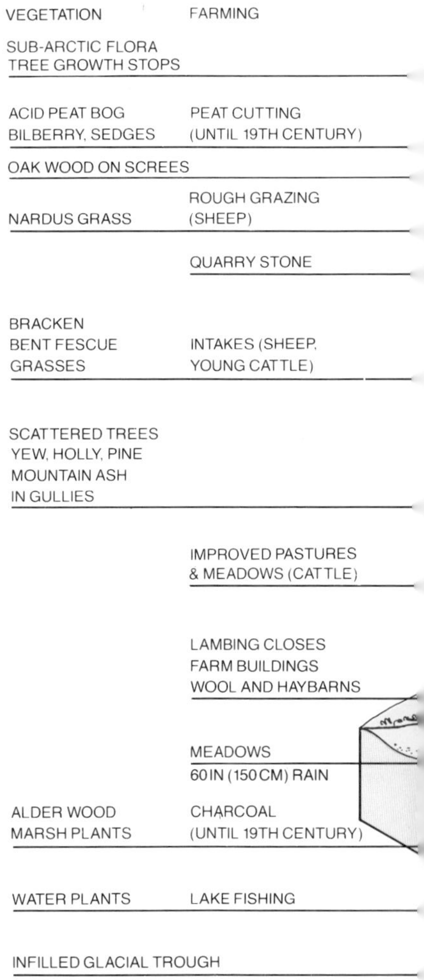

Watendlath – a Lake District hamlet with its tarn, infield enclosures, sheltering trees and, beyond, the open fell for the hill sheep.

The feudal structure of England depended upon a hierarchical arrangement by which smaller units and manors were held from the great lords in return for payments or military support. The pele towers, which are examined later in this chapter, reflect this second tier in the social hierarchy; many were the principal houses of manors, as at Broughton-in-Furness or Sizergh Castle.

Villages and Farmsteads

At the other end of the social scale was the farm unit or a collection of farms grouped, however loosely, into a settlement. These may be described as hamlets if they contained some half a dozen or more farmsteads, and villages if they had twenty or more. There was a considerable variety in the types and scales of settlement. Big, concentrated or 'nucleated' villages such as Dalston or Thursby, on the fertile farmland south-west of Carlisle, are very different in scale from the small scattered groups of buildings in the high valleys.

Kentmere, the upper section of the Kent Valley (Kentdale) north of Kendal, offers a good illustration of how the high valleys were settled. At the mouth of the narrow glaciated valley of the upper section of the River Kent is the village

Diagram of a Lake District hillside. Farms were sited on the lowest slopes of the valley sides. Meadows, cut for hay, were in the small fields round the farms and on the valley floor. Alder trees edged the lake and its fish were a valuable extra source of food. Enclosures for stock stretched up the lower slopes, and the farms in a township shared the open fell for grazing their sheep. The farms were sited near small streams for water, and outcrops of rock provided building stone. Fuel and building timber could be taken from the woodland growing on the steep scree, and additional fuel was supplied by the peat accumulating in wet hollows on the high ridges.

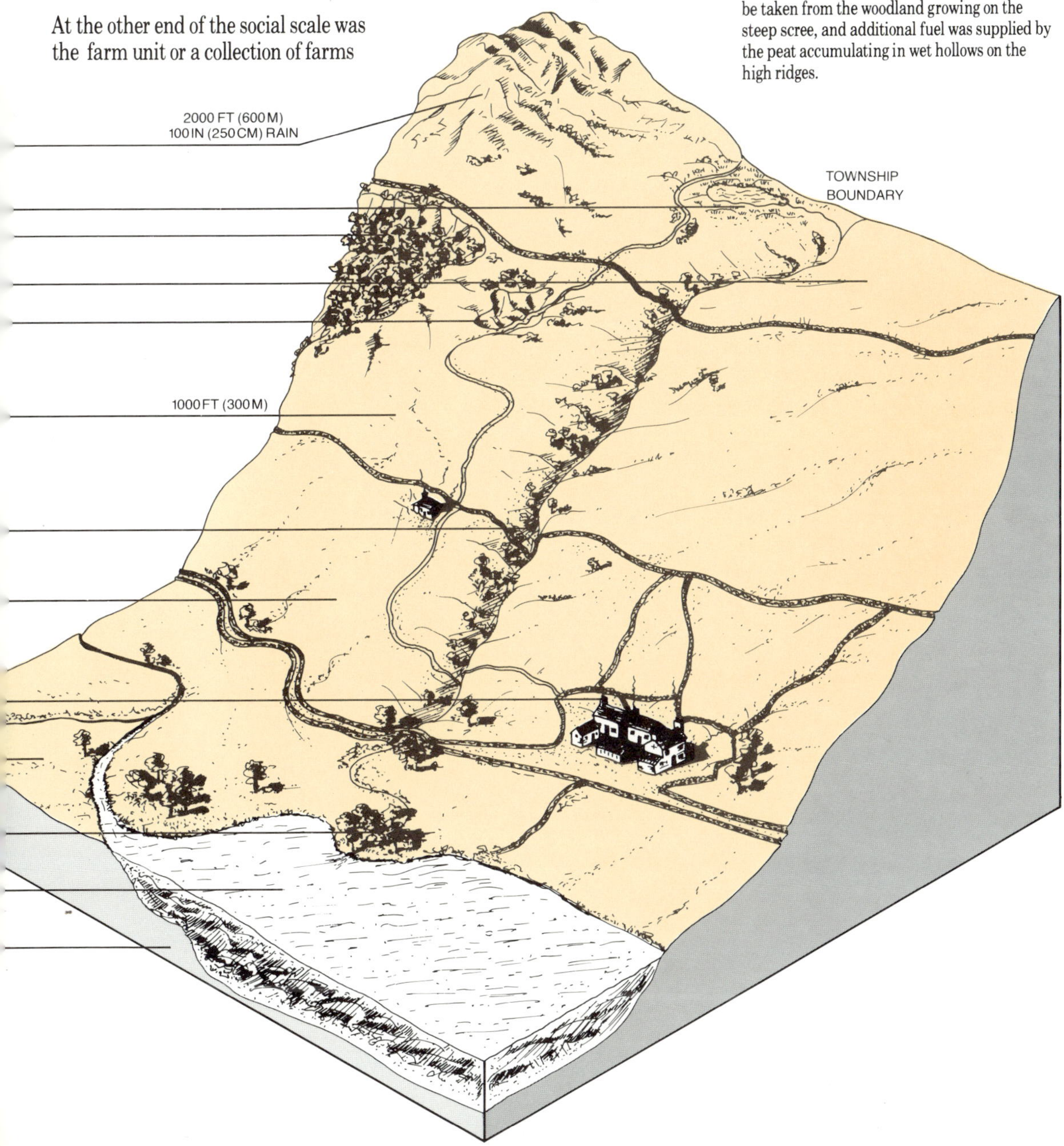

of Staveley, where the availability of water power has been an important factor in the growth of the community. Upstream from Staveley, farmsteads cling to the valley side wherever there is a suitable patch of ground next to a small tributary stream. Many of these farms have Scandinavian names and are very long-established. There was a mere or tarn in the valley bottom which gave its name to this part of the valley and which was only finally drained in the nineteenth century. (The siliceous organic deposits in the infilled lake provide a valuable raw material called diatomite which is valuable as an insulator and filler.)

At the upper end of the former mere, the valley opens out and an attractive scatter of stone-built farms is spread across its rocky, glaciated floor, set amongst a patchwork of small stone-walled fields (enclosures). Kentmere Hall, a pele tower, is the oldest standing building in the valley and is thought to have been a hunting tower in what was originally a hunting forest. Part of Kentmere settlement is called the Green Quarter and the farms there form a hamlet. Many Cumbrian settlements were divided into 'quarters' (subdivisions) for purposes of allotting common rights and other matters of local decision-making such as the amounts each occupier in the quarter should contribute to local tasks, for example the repair of roads or bridges or the taxes demanded from the valley.

To the east of Green Quarter there is a tarn called Skeggleswater and the boundary between Kentmere and Longsleddale cuts through it. The tarn lies on a flat, badly-drained plateau, and from both valleys graded tracks climb up to it. The plateau was the area from which peat was cut for the local fuel supply.

Upstream of the main area of settlement the valley closes in again, and isolated farms stretch as far as Tongue House (now in ruins). Many of the farm names are

Kentmere Hall – a fine example of a surviving pele tower situated in the middle of Kentmere, north of Kendal. It probably began life as a hunting lodge.

descriptive: Scales (a shieling or summer hut), Brockstones (badger stones), Hartrigg (the spur where deer lived) – each adds to the picture of the animal wildlife in this isolated valley head.

Power in the Parishes

So far the term 'parish' has not been used in this description of villages, hamlets and farms. A parish was an ecclesiastical unit until 1894 when civil parishes were first created. In Cumbria, the first ecclesiastical parishes developed as mother or 'minster' churches were founded. Many of these were Norman creations even if the present buildings give little clue of this. Once founded, either by a local lord or by the community, a church and its priest needed support and the payment of a tenth or 'tithe' of the annual proceeds from stock and crops became the accepted form of payment by all occupiers. This meant that boundaries had to be established between the areas paying tithe to one church and areas paying to another: thus the parishes of Cumbria evolved. Many of them, especially those which included parts of the high fells, were huge. Kendal parish included 24 'townships' (villages or hamlets) and it stretched from the top of Dunmail Raise in the north to Natland in the south.

In those early days church attendance was compulsory, and as the population grew and settlements such as Grasmere and Ambleside evolved, they were granted chapels so that the inhabitants did not have to travel too far. These chapelries were later granted full parochial status.

Dalton-in-Furness was another big medieval parish out of which Hawkshead was made a separate parish in 1578. In 1676 Colton was separated off and then, as the population increased around Windermere, the parishes of Brathay, Low Wray, Sawrey and Satterthwaite were created. The original Hawkshead parish was thus divided

into nine small parishes.

The extent and organization of the ancient parishes is nowhere more surprising than in the case of Brigham, two miles west of Cockermouth. A large sector of the north-western fells of the Lake District lay in this parish which stretched from Bassenthwaite Lake westwards to the River Marron and from the River Derwent southwards to include the whole of the Buttermere-Loweswater valley and fells. The borough of Cockermouth lay within Brigham parish and it was still only a parochial chapelry in the nineteenth century. (This meant, *inter alia,* that it did not have the right to bury its own dead.)

This arrangement reflects the relative chronology of the two settlements. Brigham, with its early Saxon place-name, existed before Cockermouth which evolved after the Castle was built in about 1150. The site was chosen by Waldeof of Dunbar as being the best from which he could control the barony of the five towns – Brigham, Eaglesfield, Dene, Greysouthern and Branthwaite – which he had been granted. From this twelfth-century land grant, the Honour and Manor of Cockermouth arose. It is difficult to understand why the new town did not have a new parish church to serve it; presumably the ecclesiastical structure was strong enough to resist any such reorganization.

The early Cumbrian parishes pre-date the establishment of the Bishopric of Carlisle. Before 1133, when the see was established, the whole area lay within the Bishopric of York and the Archdeacon of Richmond had authority over this inaccessible region as the Bishop's representative. The new Bishop built a cathedral at Carlisle, adding to the fabric of the existing Norman monastery. The bishopric was endowed with lands and with the great tithe from churches in the region. The Bishops of Carlisle had no palace there, but in the thirteenth century they built a pele tower called Rose Castle to which many later bishops have added, renewed or altered sections. Much of the present castle, on its lovely site overlooking the River Caldew, was built in the nineteenth century by Thomas Rickman, but it has older sections within the shell. The Diocese of Carlisle only extended as far south as the River Derwent. The main part of the Lake District remained in the Diocese of York until 1541 when the new Bishopric of Chester was created. In 1856 Cumbria was placed almost entirely within the Bishopric of Carlisle.

The 'Records of Kendale'

What sort of place was Cumbria after the Normans had established their castles, abbeys and churches? How did people live, what size of farms did they occupy? William Farrer extracted a great deal of information about the Kendal area in three volumes of the transcribed and translated *Records of Kendale* which were edited by J. F. Curwen and published in 1923. The details of Grasmere that he quotes serve to give at least some idea of what one Lakeland settlement was like during this period.

Grasmere was a chapelry carved out of the ancient parish of Kendal. Its church was referred to in a papal mandate of 1254 as having a rector. Pevsner describes the tower and nave as being fourteenth-century, so there may have been an earlier church on the site; there is, moreover, an unusual dedication to Saint Oswald who was King of Northumbria and died in 642.

An inquisition on the death of William de Lyndeseye showed that by 1283 he held 13 acres of arable land; 4 acres of meadow (worth two and a half times more per acre than the arable); had 15 tenants with a total of 133 acres between them; a forest rendering £3 6s 8d yearly for

View of Carlisle. The flood plain of the River Eden, the Roman and Norman fortress and the medieval market town within the walls have all shaped the city. In the nineteenth century the arrival of the main railway to Scotland and new industries all stimulated further expansion.

Above: Wasdale Head. Here in this isolated spot a small settlement, probably Viking in origin, has found just enough land on which to survive. The head of the lake has been filled in by Mosedale and Lingmell Becks and man has cleared masses of boulders into mounds and thick walls to create a network of tiny enclosures in which to grow hay and protect stock.

Left: Grasmere. This township, and the area up to the top of Dunmail Raise beyond, was part of a parish carved out of the ancient Kendal parish. It had many cloth-fulling mills in the fifteenth and sixteenth centuries that made good use of the water power from the fast-flowing local streams.

herbage (pasturage) and pannage (pasturage of pigs); a derelict fulling mill; a brewhouse; a chapel; the advowson (or right to appoint a priest), and a fishery. These returns included Langeden (modern Langdale).

In 1323 two corn mills in Grasmere were mentioned, together with a fulling mill. By 1375, after the Black Death, a rental listed 17 tenements; 7 cottages; a brewhouse; a forge; a fulling mill; a water mill, and a fishery plus three decayed tenements in Grasmere. Typical tenants were William de Wra, who held a cottage and 9 acres, and Ralph Doble who held a cottage and an 'intake', a piece of land he had taken in from the former forest or 'waste'. All of those in Grasmere and Langdale holding tenements would, of course, have important common grazing rights as well. By 1390 another survey of the occupiers of the houses shows that a smallholding of about 8 acres was typical. This was presumably 8 acres of both arable and meadow combined. A rental of 1574 listed 45 tenants with an average of about 3 acres of land described as being arable and pasture. The tenants paid £3 6s 8d a year for their pastures. This was for the 'Richmond' half of the township.

The other half of Grasmere was in the Marquis 'fee' or half of the township and totalled 48 tenants, again with about 3 acres of land each. 'The tenants within Grasmere hold a parcel of pasturable land as an improvement upon the common waste there called "les forest".' Family names occur regularly in their list: in the Marquis half of Grasmere the Grige family held 8 tenements, and the Denson family held 7 tenements in the Richmond fee.

Pele Towers

The distinctive pele towers of Cumbria were the houses of the county families or gentry rather than the homes of major national families with noted links, such as the Howards and the Cavendishes. The Stricklands of Sizergh Castle have been there since 1239 and the Flemings of Rydale, the Redmans of Levens and many others have held their estates in some instances direct from the Crown and in others from the Lords of the various baronies. These local families became prosperous through the wealth to be made from wool and cloth, and in some instances from successful and well-rewarded military service. They built solid, safe, defensible houses. (The term 'pele', covering a range of defensive structures, comes originally from *pilum*, meaning 'stake' or 'palisade'.)

The strongly built stone tower, with limited access at ground level, was an obvious solution to the problems posed by continual raids. The outbuildings were protected by a small bailey termed the 'barmkin', as seen for example at Burneside Hall with its surviving gatehouse.

Pele towers began to appear in the mid fourteenth century and were built in similar form as late as the beginning of the seventeenth century.

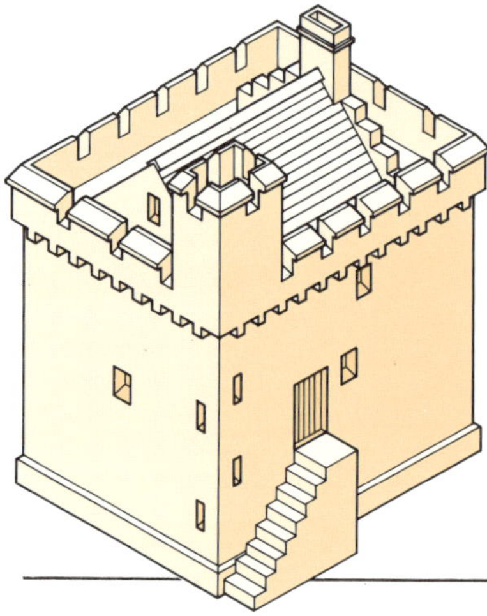

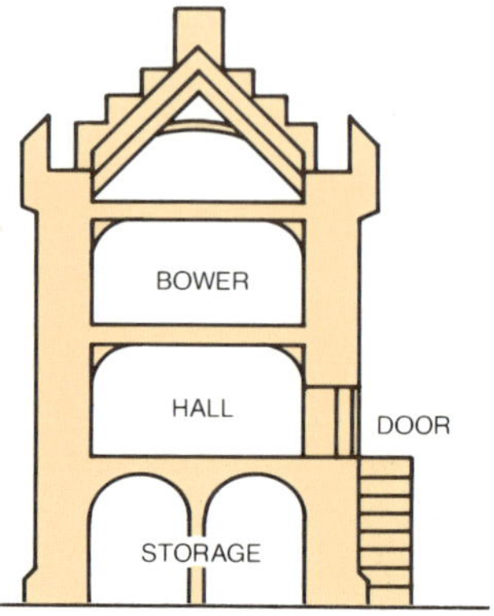

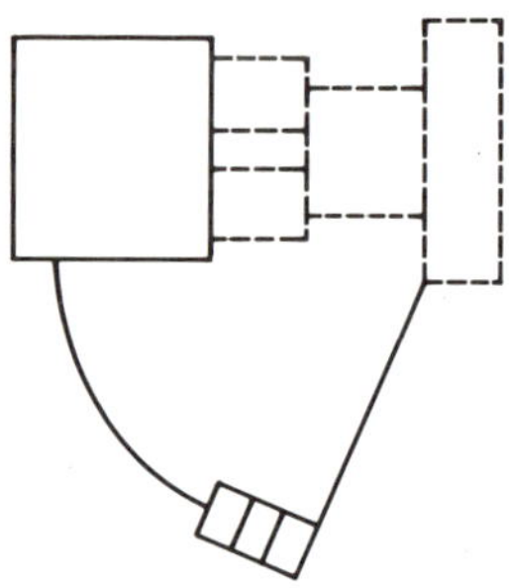

Plan of a pele tower. In the fourteenth and fifteenth centuries the lesser lords built mini-castles. These strongly-built peles were made for defence against Scottish raids and had a massive vaulted undercroft with a hall above and perhaps living accommodation above that. A courtyard or barmkin gave protection to animals inside a high wall and a gate house. As conditions became more settled, additional domestic accommodation was added in the form of a wing to the pele tower.

Sir Nikolaus Pevsner in his Cumberland and Westmorland volume in *The Buildings of England* series counted 58 pele towers in Cumberland and 31 in Westmorland. He listed several more in his North Lancashire volume as well. Sizergh Castle is owned by the National Trust and illustrates this type of building ideally. The pele tower dates from about 1340. It is a massive stone rectangle, 40ft by 60ft (12m by 18m) with walls nearly 10ft (3m) thick at the base. When conditions became a little more peaceful a hall was added. As with any such important building, it has been modified a number of times. In the Elizabethan period the interior acquired its outstanding quality, with five beautifully carved chimney pieces and much good furniture.

Nearby Levens Hall, now

Sizergh Castle, a fine example of a pele tower, built c.1340 and owned for several centuries by the Strickland family. It is now a National Trust property.

home of the Bagot family, has a similar core to the later buildings that developed around it, and at Broughton-in-Furness a splendid, massive tower is hidden behind a Gothic Revival façade.

A smaller house type, known as the 'bastle', seems to represent the response at a slightly lower social level to the unsettled political conditions of north-east Cumberland. Bastle houses are in effect a raised hall with quarters for animals below, so arranged that invaders could not easily walk in. The architectural historian R. W. Brunskill argues that their very modesty of scale may have made them less attractive to raiders than the better defended pele towers.

The Medieval Market Place

Castles and pele towers were frequently associated with another very important new element in the late twelfth- and early thirteenth-century countryside: the market place. The lords of baronies or their sub-tenants secured from the Crown market charters allowing markets to be held, and often fairs as well. Many of them laid out new settlements with the market area as their centre-piece. Appleby was laid out by Ranulph de Meschines, with its market to the north of the castle. Penrith, for a period under royal patronage, had a corn market and two stock market areas – Sandgate and Great Dockray. Kendal was the first town in the region to secure a dated charter, in 1189, which also gave permission to hold three fairs. Nearly four hundred years later it became a borough by gift of Queen Elizabeth I. The other surviving market towns gained their charters in the thirteenth century – Millom, Dalton, Egremont, Keswick, Ulverston and Carlisle.

Now consider another group of places, whose present size and status well reflect the changing importance of settlements as time

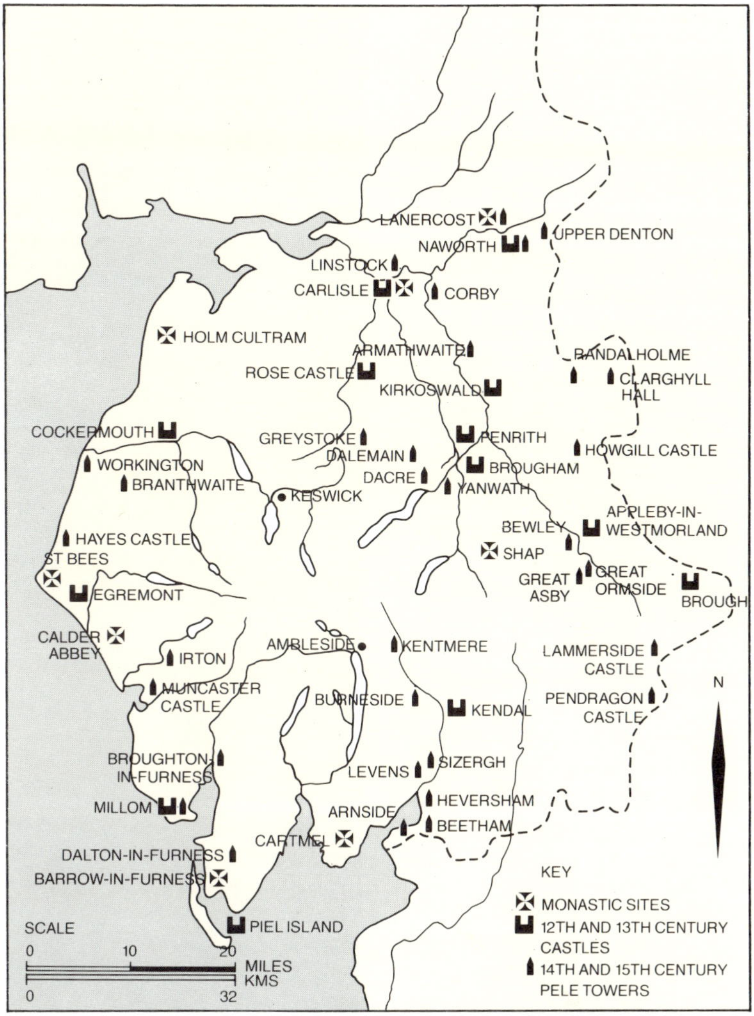

Map showing the monastic foundations, castles and pele towers in the Lake District and its neighbouring regions.

Keswick market place. Keswick became an important copper-mining centre in the sixteenth century. The old parish church is at Crosthwaite and the new one was not built in Keswick until 1838, by which time the town had become a growing tourist centre. The Town Hall, with its tower, was built in 1813.

goes on. Who would suspect that Ireby, Flookburgh, Newton Arlosh, Staveley, Bootle and Ravenglass were once all markets? Careful examination of their layout, for example the wide 'street' in Ravenglass, shows evidence of an original market place. Hesket Newmarket tells its own story from its name and it still has a wide long green in its centre which began as a market place. Perhaps even more surprising is the fact that Shap village had a market charter awarded in 1687. The village's long street must have been very difficult to move through on market day as the stock were brought in from the surrounding fells.

The examples of property holdings in Grasmere in the fourteenth century referred to earlier mentioned corn mills, a fulling mill and a forge. All of these were dependent on water for their power. By the thirteenth century there were water-powered corn mills on many Cumbrian streams, especially in the lower valleys.

The fulling process relates to the cloth trade, and wool and cloth have long played a very important role in Cumbrian life. Much of the land was fit only for sheep, which formed a major source of income both to the abbeys and to other landowners. The famous breed of the Lake District is the Herdwick. This is a small, thick-woolled, white-faced sheep, the origins of which are unclear but it is a long-established Lakeland breed which can stand bad weather and stays on its own 'heaf' or patch of ground. Flocks are to this day sold along with the farm to which they belong.

Although the wool was moderate in quality, Kendal and Cartmel cloths were well known in the early medieval period. The women spun and wove and the men also wove on all fell farms. The cloth had to be finished by being matted or felted and this process, known as fulling, was carried out from a very early date with the aid of hammers driven by water. By 1453 Grasmere parish had six fulling mills and by the early sixteenth century it had eighteen.

The iron industry has already been referred to as an important source of income to Furness Abbey and it became a major industry later. Many bloomeries (small charcoal-fuelled furnaces) were erected, especially by the Cistercian monks in the Coniston Water area. There is some doubt about how early water power was used to drive hammers or to enable reheated iron from the bloomeries to be worked more carefully, but the Grasmere survey of 1375 does mention a forge, and presumably it was powered by water.

Lead, copper and silver

Top: Ruins of Furness Abbey, founded in 1127 by Savignac monks who about twenty years later joined the Cistercians. The surviving parts of the church nave and transepts date from the twelfth and thirteenth centuries. Also to be seen are the remains of the infirmary and the abbot's lodging.
Above: Wool has always been a major source of income to Cumbrian farms. Herdwick sheep, here represented by a ewe and her lambs, are a distinctive Lake District breed.

magnificent walk from Rydal over Heron Pike and Rydal Fell to Fairfield and back down High Pike follows a massive, if now crumbling, wall for most of the route with an outer ditch over much of its length; this wall enclosed Rydale, a perfect natural park on the Fleming estate. In 1090 William II created a big Royal deer park at Plumpton Hay, just to the south of Carlisle.

On a larger scale still, there were the stretches of forest. Again the names survive: Skiddaw Forest, for example, covers one of the largest stretches of inaccessible fell in the Lake District to the north of Skiddaw. Inglewood Forest, south of Carlisle, was perhaps the largest stretch of late-surviving forest in Cumbria. In 1300 it stretched from the Riven Eden at its confluence with the Eamont to Carlisle along the Roman road to the River Wampool, and then back up that stream and the Chalk Beck round the east side of the Skiddaw massif and back to Penrith. This was the largest royal hunting forest.

'Forest' in this context is a legal term implying that Forest Law, the severe laws relating to the rights of hunting, applied to the area. These rights could be given by the Crown to great Lords, as at Copeland in west Cumberland, or held directly by the King, as at Inglewood. Although hunting remained a major concern at Inglewood, settlement was not prevented and the new parish of Sebergham was created complete with a new parish church in the 1280s. However, large stretches of unenclosed tracts of this forest did survive until the Parliamentary Enclosure Award of 1819 finally abolished them.

As the area became more peaceful, as the population grew and the income from cattle and sheep became important to landowners, so the expanses of parks and forests were much reduced. The Dissolution of the huge monastic estates tended to speed up these processes of land reorganization.

ores were worked in the early Middle Ages in Cumbria, but it was the post-Dissolution period that saw a real expansion in these activities. The Alston mines were being worked for their silver from 1130, and Garrigill may have been the main centre. King Edward III (1327–77) appointed Robert de Barton keeper of silver lead mines at Silver Beck and Minersdale: the latter mines were almost certainly in the Upper Caldew Valley behind Skiddaw. The famous Goldscope copper mines near Keswick were also worked from the early thirteenth century and in 1474 King Edward IV appointed a commission to inquire into the mines of Alston and Keswick.

Parks and Forests

By the 1530s, when the Dissolution of the Monasteries took place, many forms of economic activity were already under way in Cumbria. There were, however, large areas to which development came late or had not even begun because they had the status of parks or forests.

The right to empark an area was a right granted by the Crown and it usually went with other considerable privileges, such as the right to castellate a building (turn it into a castle). Naworth Park, about eight miles north-east of Carlisle, is a good example. Although there are records of Anglo-Saxon parks, most seem to appear first in the thirteenth century as landowners sought permission to keep their own herds of deer for hunting. They were fenced with large banks and ditches and often had a hunting lodge; some of these later became known as the parkhouse or park farm. The parks of the Abbots of Furness have already been mentioned, but many lay lords had such parks. The names Park Farm and Troutbeck Park are still shown on the map and the stout walls of the deer park can be seen at the head of the Troutbeck Valley that leads to the Kirkstone Pass. The

THE STATESMEN AND THE MINERS

In Cumbria as elsewhere, the Dissolution of the Monasteries by Henry VIII between 1535 and 1542 was an event of great importance. Many thousand acres of monastic estates came on the land market. It is generally recognized that this was a progressive move – at least to those who managed in one way or another to secure some of the former monastic lands. A petition from the people of Furness to King Henry, pleading that he should not dissolve the Abbey, stressed how inhabitants of Furness benefited from the many services provided by it. They had, for example, a weekly allocation of 'thirty dozen of coarse wheat bread from the Abbey kitchens' while their children received a good education from the monks.

Many of the granges, dairy farms, stock farms and iron bloomeries that had been established from the end of the thirteenth century had become properties held on family tenancies. The King, who was keen to encourage a loyal land-owning population in Cumbria as an effective check to potential Scottish attacks, allowed many of these tenants to become virtual freeholders of their properties. Thus was born that distinctive 'aristocracy' of the Lake District known as the 'statesmen'. These families, some based in their slate-built farmsteads and some in their older pele towers, became the key figures in Lakeland society until the Lakes became the focus of the early tourist industry and an immigrant population of aesthetes moved in to contemplate beauty rather than to drive their sheep along the wet hillsides.

How did the settlements that existed by the 1530s manage their lands and how did they establish which stretches of fell belonged to whom? Land grants, such as those mentioned in the previous chapter, defined the feudal baronies, honours and manors. Townships were not manors yet may have long regarded certain outlying lands as theirs. For example, a map of Hartsop made in the eighteenth century notes that the men of Ambleside were prone to take peat from Hartsop land. As was stressed in the first chapter, most lakeland communities had the natural boundaries of the crests of high ridges, the middle of swift flowing streams or shore of a lake to define their territories.

Within these territories, as at Hartsop, some land was used for crops and was probably cropped every year. Such lands, lying close to the settlement, were 'infields' and their fertility was maintained by regular manuring with dung from the byres or hoghouses (sheephouses). Rye and oats would be grown on the infields.

As well as an infield in which the commoners of a community would hold land there would also be hay meadows in which they had allocated portions as well. Grassland has always been of critical importance to a region where cereals do not naturally do well and it has always been the hay crop that has determined the head of stock that can survive the winter. Areas of 'doled' meadows usually lay on the valley bottoms and on any flat land near the streams.

Brampton, a large parish with an attractive market town in its centre, was described in detail in an early seventeenth-century survey. 'The Lord hath a faire stone house at the east end of the town called the Hallhouse, composed about with the common waie or street.' Eleven more houses stretched from the hallhouse to the beck, and north of the beck were four more houses.

Most of the holdings described were between twenty-five and thirty acres in size with crofts and closes around them – both these terms being used to define the small fields near the houses. The illustration shows the major components of the parish of Brampton as they were in

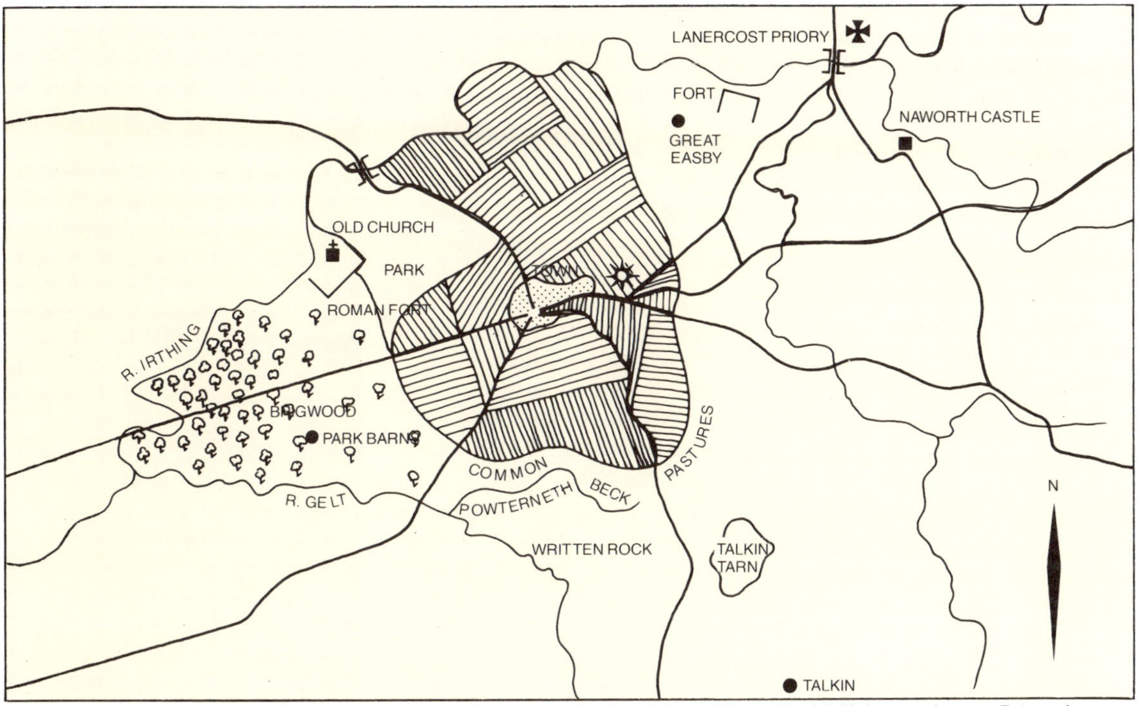

Map of Brampton, where a small market town replaced the earlier settlement by the old church. The medieval fields lay near the town. Brigwood provided building timber and fuel. A wide stretch of common land from the south-west of the town, reaching round to the south-east, provided grazing for cattle and sheep. Talkin Tarn was an important fishery. The Dacre family gradually created a park in the east of the parish around Naworth Castle.

1603. Naworth Park, in which the castle lay, covered 442 acres. In the west of the parish Brigwood, presumably the 'wood by the bridge', was huge and stretched over 712 acres. The best timber was at the west end of the wood, probably because the inhabitants of Brampton had made inroads on the timber near the town. Another park lay north of Brigwood. The common pastures on which the people of Brampton could graze their stock extended in an arc from the River Gelt to the south-west through to the south and east of the town and covered 1300 acres, stretching to Talkin Tarn at their extreme south-east. The arable and meadow land lay immediately to the west and to the north of the town.

The Brampton that now exists was a New Town laid out by the lords of the Barony of Gilsland and the first record of its market charter is in 1252. The Norman parish church was built inside the walls of a Roman fort overlooking the River Irthing and it lay a mile to the north and west of the present town, which may have replaced the earlier settlement. The new chapel incorporated much material from the old church when it was built in 1788. It was noted in 1829 that the courts for 'the Great Barony of Gilsland' were held in Brampton. Naworth Castle, 'the baronial mansion of the Great Barony of Gilsland', was a Dacre stronghold and then descended to the Howard family who were later to build their main house at Castle Howard in Yorkshire.

Professor W. G. Hoskins has written of the 'Great Rebuilding' of English farmhouses that took place after about 1580. In Cumbria this process also took place but it happened later, in the mid seventeenth century. The castles, churches and pele towers were stone-built from Norman times onwards, but there is a less certain picture about the building materials used in the farmhouses and cottages.

J. B. Bradbury, describing Cockermouth, noted that for centuries its only stone building was the castle. Other houses were built on a wooden frame, the walls of wattle and daub, clay or turf and the roofs of turf, rushes or heather. Gradually, cobbles taken from the rivers and fields replaced other walling materials and remains of these are often revealed when cottages are modernized; but the use of thatch persisted. Other writers have also implied that stone was used later, replacing the earlier timber or wattle and daub.

Many early Cumbrian buildings may have had stone walls that were not load-bearing but were simply fenced in a 'cruck' type of timber-frame construction. From there, builders progressed to using 'raised crucks' and making stone walls that were load-bearing.

Three levels of post-medieval building can be recognized: the larger houses, many of which grew up between 1550 and 1700 from cores containing an earlier pele tower; the smaller houses, probably belonging to 'statesmen' and built in a local style between perhaps 1550 at the very earliest and about 1800, and cottages which only really developed in the eighteenth century when a variety of new jobs – for quarrymen, miners and millworkers – began to appear. Farm buildings are commonly associated with the larger houses and all sorts of interesting industrial buildings often explain the existence of the cottages which were built nearby.

Any group of Cumbrian farm buildings will almost certainly have undergone many changes during its history, so that earlier forms may have almost completely given way to newer.

The most famous of the statesmen's houses in Cumbria is Townend in Troutbeck, now a National Trust property. It was, until 1942, the home of the Browne family. It is a complicated building with four ground-floor elements: the main living room (known as the 'house' or 'firehouse') with the great fireplace; the cross passage (or 'hallan'), and the kitchen (or 'downhouse') with another chimney stack. The dairy, curator's wing and bower were probably added later. George Browne, who built the original part of the house c.1626, was a wealthy sheep farmer and his wool barn was on the opposite side of the road from the house.

Townend – a statesman's house built c.1626 and now owned by the National Trust. The Browne family were sheep farmers and several generations contributed to the building and furnishing of this attractive house. On the other side of the road are the wool barns.

Townend interior, showing the 'firehouse', as the living room was known, with its long low window facing south and an abundance of ornate carving carried out by various members of the Browne family in the seventeenth and eighteenth centuries.

Spinning Gallery, Townend. In the great wool barns of the Browne family, fleeces were stacked until the wool was sold to the local spinner and to merchants. The Spinning Gallery, linking the two wings, may have been put to uses other than spinning; possibly fleeces were dried there. (This part of the building is not open to the public.)

Early Industry

In the opening chapter we described the complex geological history of the Lake District. The mineral veins that were forced through the bedrock cooled at different rates and altered and replaced many types of rock. This meant that a wide range of minerals and metals was created, many of considerable economic value.

Iron ore was probably the most important mineral of all. It occurs as a 'replacement ore', rather than as a vein mineral, and therefore it has been worked on the surface and in greater masses than the other metal ores. Iron was smelted by the monks of Furness Abbey or their tenants from 1300 onwards. Small hearths were established on exposed hillsides where supplies of charcoal were available. The hearths, or 'bloomeries', were inefficient and much iron-rich clinker can be found near the smelting sites. The path from the south end of Coniston Water to Ickenthwaite, for example, has much clinker and ore scattered along it and a smelting site lies just to the west of Ickenthwaite.

The lumps of partially smelted ore were next taken to forges where they could be reheated and purified to the point at which the metal could be hammered into swords or ploughshares. Large quantities of charcoal were needed for this process and the woods were rapidly felled.

By the sixteenth century, water was being used to power bellows in the final stages of purifying the metal and to drive the hammers in the forges. Water wheels were set in fast-flowing streams such as the Crake at Spark Bridge and Cunsey Beck between Esthwaite Water and Windermere. By the late seventeenth century, coke was being used in the first blast furnace, established at Coalbrookdale in Shropshire and founded by Abraham Darby I. The Coalbrookdale technology was slow to spread northwards, and families such as the Wilkinsons at Backbarrow did not begin to use coke in their furnaces until after 1800. The energy from the River Leven was still used to drive their bellows, and Backbarrow became a key site when the earlier and later technologies met.

The furnace there remained at work until the late 1950s, surviving as a working piece of industrial archaeology producing 'pigs' of various qualities of iron that were stacked in the yard until a customer with particular requirements came along. The coke arrived by the Furness Railway. Workmen wheeled barrow loads of Swedish ore and Durham coke along a gantry and tipped them by hand into the little furnace. This is potentially one of the most interesting of all the industrial sites of the Lake District.

Another important mining

An overshot water wheel in the Coniston Valley. This probably drove machinery that crushed the copper ore.

The slate wharf, Clappersgate, near Ambleside. Slate from Langdale was shipped from here along Lake Windermere for local use and to the coast.

activity was for copper. In the sixteenth century Queen Elizabeth I brought in a group of German miners from Augsburg to exploit the copper known to exist near Keswick. Their main agent was Daniel Hochstetter and the Queen established The Society for the Mines Royal to encourage the work. The main copper mines were in the Newlands Valley, where the Goldscope Mine was the major site, and in Borrowdale just upstream of the head of Derwent Water. Brigham, now a suburb of Keswick, was the site of the smelter and the River Greta provided the water power for driving the crushing hammers and bellows. By the late sixteenth century, The Society for the Mines Royal and the German miners had also begun to work the copper ores to the west of Coniston up Church Beck.

The copper mining area to the north-west of Coniston bears the scars and traces of mining as much as any part of the Lake District. The major water-powered crushing, refining and smelting plants lay up Church Beck. A maze of mine shafts and adits riddles the fells between Church Beck and Tilberthwaite Gill to the east. Thirteen water wheels were at work on the Beck in the mid nineteenth century, when production was at its peak. The whole massif of the Coniston Fells was mineralized and there are many signs of other workings, such as those in the Seathwaite Tarn and Greenburn Beck valleys. The level of Levers Water was raised and Greenburn Reservoir was created in order to produce a steady head of water for the industrial sites downstream. The Church Beck area has now been tidied up but interesting interpretative work is being done there, and amateur geologists and mineralogists can comb some of the old mining tips for the distinctive green-tinged pieces of copper ore (malachite) and their associated minerals.

A quite different mining area, already briefly referred to in the previous chapter, is the lead-mining region around Alston, away on Cumbria's eastern edge. In their study of Cumbria, Millward and Robinson give an interesting account of how one company, the London Lead Company, built a completely new settlement, Nenthead, in the Nent Valley which joins the valley of the South Tyne at Alston. The Company received its Charter in 1692; it was Quaker-owned and it looked after its expanding workforce. By 1766 there were 119 mines, the Rampsgill Vein being particularly rich. The miners became small farmers as well, and kept some cattle and sheep despite the difficult climate of the high Pennines. A final burst of prosperity in 1849–50 was followed by decline, and despite later attempts to work zinc ores, the mining activities of the area finally died, leaving many traces of the old workings as a reminder of the industrial past in those high fells.

Another interesting and unusual mining area occurs in a little-visited part of the region. The valley of the River Caldew cuts deeply into the Skiddaw massif and the river makes a sharp eastwards bend at Ordnance Survey map reference 327325. At this point it exposes one of the most varied geological outcrops of the whole region. The geologist will find a wide range of granophyres and gabbros in the stream bed and on the mine waste. Wolfram, an ore of tungsten used in strengthening metals, is the ore mined.

The most characteristic Lake District rock is slate. It has been used as a building stone for all the major buildings of the region. Green's early paintings of Ambleside suggest that the smaller cottages were still being built of timber, wattle and daub and roofed with turf until the mid nineteenth century, when an entirely new, neat slate style began to appear in the mushrooming hotels and boarding houses. Each settlement had its own quarry in a nearby field or on the local fell.

It was, however, the arrival of the railway – at Shap in 1846, at Windermere in 1849 and at Coniston in 1859 – that made the slate accessible to a much wider market at just the time when the industrial towns were rapidly expanding. The distinctive green Lakeland slate was used to roof many a new house in the north-western manufacturing towns. The landscape of Honister Pass, and especially of the Tilberthwaite area,

Above: Slate quarrying has scarred the landscape in several areas. This is Bowder Stone Quarry, near Derwent Water.

Above: Slate for building, at Bridge House, Ambleside.
Right: Slate workers' cottages at Elterwater. Their style is typical of cottages built in the nineteenth century in the Lake District.
Below left: The Old Quarry at Rosthwaite, in Borrowdale. Old slate workings gradually merged with the surrounding landscape as weather and vegetation modified their sharp outlines.

bears bleak witness to the growth of a Lakeland industry which has recently recovered from a period of decline.

The Elterwater quarries have virtually created new markets, notably for fireplaces and slate cladding, and the development of the National Park with its more rigorous building regulations concerning local materials has meant that slate is booming again. The Elterwater showrooms and processing plants are well worth a visit. The Kirkstone Pass has new quarries on its south side working a noticeably green form of slate. Two other valleys in which mining and quarrying were important secondary activities are Kentmere and Longsleddale. The Wren Gill quarry site at the head of Longsleddale has a remarkably well-preserved ridged road up to the quarry which enabled the horses and their heavy slate wagons to negotiate the slope. This quarry was at its peak of production in the late nineteenth century, but now seems more a part of the natural scenery rather than of the man-made landscape.

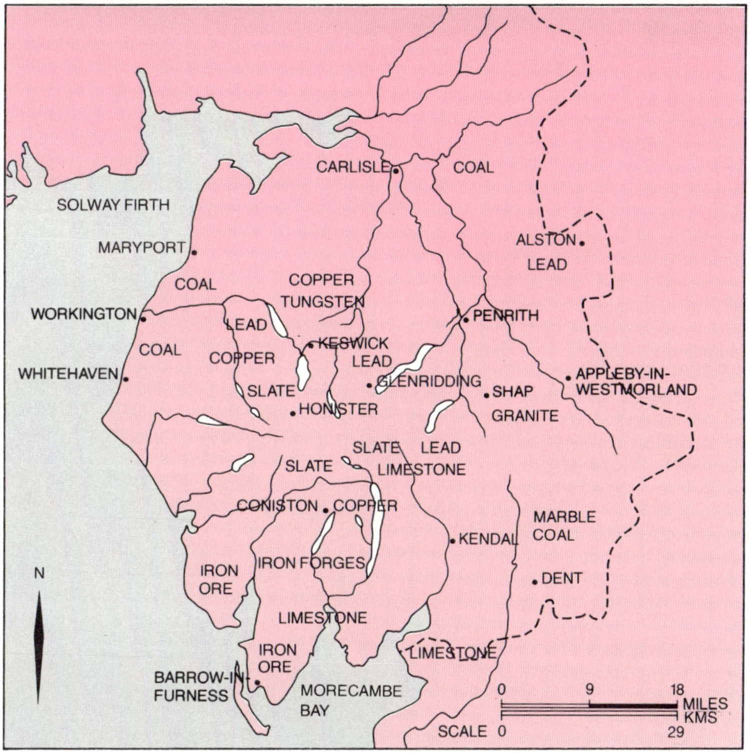

Industrial map of the region. The ancient rocks of Cumbria have a complex history and contain many useful minerals. These, together with the power derived from the fast-flowing streams, have given rise to several phases of industrial development.

THE EIGHTEENTH CENTURY

Daniel Defoe visited the north-west of England around 1720. In a very down-to-earth commentary he saw 'Westmorland a county eminent only for being the wildest, most barren and frightful of any . . . in England'. He described Appleby as 'once a flourishing city, now a scattering, decayed and half-demolished town, the fatal effects of the ancient inroads of the Scots . . . who several times were masters of this town, and at length burnt it to the ground, which blow it has not yet recovered'.

He was more pleased with the Eden Valley and with Penrith and Carlisle and he cut across to the west coast where he noticed that Whitehaven was growing rapidly. At Cockermouth he commented on the wealth of salmon in the River Derwent and the way in which fresh salmon went from Workington and Carlisle (presumably, in the latter case, salmon from the River Eden) by relays of fast horses to London. He also noted that copper had been mined in the Derwent Fells but that the mines were not economic in the early years of the century.

Age of the Picturesque

In the second half of the eighteenth century a new public attitude developed towards the Lake District. It was no longer viewed as an area off the beaten track where a sparsely scattered population earned a hard living rearing sheep and cattle and winning copper, lead and slate from the mountain gullies. This was not so much because of changes that were taking place amongst Lakeland folk but because outsiders were discovering the picturesque qualities of the landscape.

The Picturesque movement has been defined by P. Bicknell as the 'art of cooking nature' and as occupying the transition from the Classically ordered world of Claude and the Augustan poets to the Romantic visions of Constable and Wordsworth. It was a new aesthetic and it led, first, to the 'discovery' of the Lake District, and later to the 'opening up' of the whole area of Cumbria.

Dr John Brown of St John's College, Cambridge, writing to Lord

Crummock Water, north-west of Buttermere – a beautiful 2½-mile lake from which the River Cocker flows north to meet the Derwent at Cockermouth.

Above: Rosthwaite Pack-horse Bridge. By the second half of the eighteenth century people began to look at the lakes and rivers not just as functional sources of fish and power, and at the mountains as hindrances, but also to admire them for their aesthetic benefits.

Below: Late eighteenth-century enclosures at Rosthwaite in Borrowdale. This landscape of hedged and walled fields was evolving during the years when the Lake District was becoming more popular with outsiders.

Above: View of Borrowdale, sketched in 1806 by John Constable (1776–1837), which makes a fine impressionistic portrait of the valley.
Below: Francis Towne (1740–1816) brought out the shape and structure of Raven Cragg, above Thirlmere (before it was a reservoir) in a surprisingly modern way in this water colour painted in 1786.

Lyttelton in 1753, explained that 'the full perfection of Keswick consists of three circumstances, Beauty, Horror, Immensity united. But to give you a complete idea of these three perfections as they are joined in Keswick would require the united powers of Claude, Salvator and Poussin . . .' Dr Brown visited the Lake District annually as 'a religious act' and his much-quoted letter to Lord Lyttelton was printed in part in many of the early Lake District publications.

The Reverend William Gilpin was described as having been the most dedicated traveller in search of the picturesque. He made a number of tours of England's wild places between 1769 and 1774 which he himself illustrated. His friends included Thomas Gray and Horace Walpole. The visits by this group and others began the avalanche of 'dons, divines and dilettanti' that descended on the lakes. The topographical artists of this period created a print-selling industry, and William Westall's illustrations for *Views of the Lake and Vale of Keswick* are prime

Above: Keswick, drawn c.1820 by William Westall (1781–1850). The then compact town is shown with Latrigg to the north-east.
Below: Thomas Gray (1716–71), one of the earliest to come to the Lake District in search of the picturesque. Gray visited the Lakes in 1769 and 'passed six days Lap'd in Elysium'. His *Journal of the Lakes* was written in 1769 and published in 1775.

examples of this early phase of popularization.

If the attitude of the outside world to this barren corner of England was changing, so was the countryside itself – except in the areas of high fell where conditions discouraged any attempts to improve the land. In many parishes at the beginning of the century the infield or town field was still to a great extent a common arable field in which owners and tenants had a few strips (riggs). This entitled them to graze cattle and sheep on the common pastures of the parish.

People gradually realized that it was more efficient to have all the arable land of one holding together, and occupiers began to assemble pieces of the common field and put a hedge and wall round them, thereby enclosing a piece of the common for their own use. Similarly, the grazing of animals could be better controlled if the common pastures or waste was divided up between individuals; so the pressure to enclose the common pastures also increased. These commons not only provided grazing but also fuel from peat and furze; stone, clay and gravel for buildings and roads, and timber for fuel and for building.

From the mid eighteenth century, as Parliamentary procedures and legislation developed, a systematic approach to the process of enclosing common fields and wastes was established, and landowners increasingly turned to the Parliamentary process to enclose these ancient areas of common land rather than to the older piecemeal local arrangements. New roads were laid out, hundreds of miles of stone walls were built, and new farms appeared as wide stretches of formerly common land became privately owned.

Despite a general speeding-up in the process of enclosure in the second half of the eighteenth century, Eden in his *State of the Poor* of 1795 noted negatively how at Hesket 'no more than 200 acres have been inclosed within the last 50 years. A large part appears to have had its hedges planted a little before that period.' He also commented that, at Croglin, although enclosed land was more valuable than unenclosed, 'only about 100 acres of common fields have been enclosed within the last 50 years but a great part of the arable land still remains in narrow crooked dales or "ranes" as they are called.' At Cumrow things were still very primitive. 'The land is cultivated in the old Cumberland manner. The grass ridges in the fields are from 20 to 30 feet wide and some of them are 1000 feet in length. Grazing of cattle often injures the crops.'

Whilst Wordsworth wrote

Above: William Wordsworth (1770–1850). Born at Cockermouth, he went to school at Hawkshead. After Cambridge he returned to the Lake District to Dove Cottage, Grasmere (1799–1808), Allen Bank, Grasmere (1808–11), Grasmere Parsonage (1811–13), and Rydal Mount, Rydal (1813–50).
Above right: Dorothy Wordsworth (1771–1855), William's sister. She lived with William and his wife, Mary, for much of their lives. Her journal of 1800–03 gives both a detailed record of their lives and also a beautifully written contemporary account of the Lake District.
Above far right: View of Castle Crag, by Julius Caesar Ibbetson (1757–1817). Born at Masham in Yorkshire, Ibbetson settled at Rydal between 1798 and 1803 and painted some delightful Romantic views.

so romantically of the Lake District and was, indeed, the prime influence in its popularization, it is worth noting that the words iron, coal, industry, mines, lead and copper were not mentioned in the index to his *Guide through the Lakes* (originally written in 1810). Although he does deplore 'the inventions and universal applications of machinery' as having removed the second income of weaving and knitting from Lakes farmsteads, he says nothing of the industrial smoke and fire that so fascinated painters such as Joseph Wright.

It was a romanticized idyll that Wordsworth conjured up, and that is what everyone still appears to expect when they first arrive at Grasmere – though it is unlikely that visitors to the area will ever again find it. Nowhere does the poet's romanticizing of 'this perfect Republic' appear to better effect than in the following extract from his *Guide*:

'Thus has been given a faithful description the minuteness of which the reader will pardon, of the face of this country as it was, and had been through centuries, till within the last sixty years. Towards the head of these Dales was found a perfect Republic of Shepherds and Agriculturists, among whom the plough of each man was confined to the maintenance of his own family, or to the occasional accommodation of his neighbour. Two or three cows furnished each family with milk and cheese. The chapel was the only edifice that presided over these dwellings, the supreme head of this pure Commonwealth; the members of which existed in the midst of a powerful empire like an ideal society or an organised community, whose constitution had been imposed and regulated by the mountains which protected it. Neither high-born nobleman, knight, nor esquire was here; but many of these humble sons of the hills had a consciousness that the land, which they walked over and tilled, had for more than five hundred years been possessed by men of their name and blood; and venerable was the transition, when a curious traveller, descending from the heart of the mountains, had come to some ancient manorial residence in the more open parts of the Vales, which, through the rights attached to its proprietor, connected the almost visionary mountain republic he had been contemplating with the substantial frame of society as existing in the laws and constitution of a mighty empire.'

Wordsworth's sister Dorothy kept a journal which is in many ways more fascinating than her brother's guide. Dorothy's *Grasmere Journals* lasted only from 1800–03. Her literary sketches of the area near Dove Cottage at the turn of the century are worth a score of drier fragments. For example, on 16 June 1800: 'The vale of little Langdale looked bare and unlovely. Collath was wild and interesting from the peat carts and peat gatherers – the valley all perfumed with Gale [bog myrtle] and wild thyme. The woods about the waterfall veined with rich yellow Broom. A succession of delicious views from Skelleth to Brathay ... we drank tea at Mr Ibbetson's [the painter Julius Caesar Ibbetson, living in Clappersgate] and returned to Ambleside.'

She packed so many observations into one outing. On another walk with William, from Brotherswater to Ambleside on Good Friday 16 April 1802, they reached the foot of Brotherswater and then Dorothy 'left William sitting on the Bridge and went along the path on the right side of the Lake through the wood. The water under the boughs of the bare old trees, the simplicity of the mountains and the exquisite beauty of the path. There was one grey cottage ... when I returned I found William writing a poem descriptive of the sights and sounds we saw and heard ['The Cock is Crowing']. There was the gentle flowing of the stream, the glittering lively lake, green fields without a living creature to be seen on them, behind us a flat pasture with 42 cattle feeding to our left, the road leading to the hamlet, no smoke there, the sun shone on the bare roofs. The people were at work ploughing, harrowing and sowing – lasses spreading dung, a dog's barking now and then, cocks crowing, birds twittering, the snow in patches on the top of the highest hills, yellow palms, purple and green twigs on the Birches, ashes with their glittering spikes quite bare. We then ... passed two sisters ... one with two pitch forks in her hand. The other had a spade.'

She also wrote of seeing hundreds of cattle in the vale up to the foot of the Kirkstone Pass. Her exceptionally observant reactions bring us a valuable portrait of the Lake District as it was nearly two hundred years ago.

Although Wordsworth does not mention industry and commerce in his *Guide* they were implicit in Lakeland life. In 1777, for example, Hugh Tyson, husband of Ann Tyson, William's Hawkshead landlady, was involved in the sale of charcoal for a Mr Stephen Green of Surrey, to the Backbarrow Iron Company. He sold 13 dozen and ten sacks of coal for

Lowther Street, Whitehaven. Lowther Street was the principal axial street of the new town and it still contains many fine eighteenth-century buildings.

£27 13s 4d. He paid several workmen for charcoal preparation – for example, Edward Braithwaite £5 11s 9d for 'Coling [i.e. making charcoal from wood] and Peeling Barke'.

The Coalfield and its Ports

The eighteenth century also saw the development of the small Cumberland Coalfield and its associated towns and ports. The coalfield stretched from Wigton to south of Whitehaven in a narrow belt between the older rocks of the Lake District to the south-east and the New Red Sandstones of the Solway Plain to the north and west. A major fault terminates the coalfield at St Bees Head. The coal seams dip seawards and a number of the old collieries ran out under the Irish Sea, so increasing the difficulties of working seams that were comparatively thin and faulted compared with those in the bigger English coalfields.

Three families – the Senhouses at Maryport, the Lowthers at Whitehaven and the Curwens at Workington – were responsible for the growth of the three coalfield ports. The Lowthers had received the monastic estates of St Bees Abbey at the Dissolution in the 1530s. In 1636, when only nine or ten thatched cottages existed by the inlet, Christopher Lowther built a short quay at Whitehaven and this increased the coal exports sharply. Sir John Lowther, having had a grant of land from King Charles II in 1666, laid out a completely new rectangular town to the north of the small settlement. He built St Nicholas's Church in 1693 on the site of an earlier chapel (this was rebuilt in 1883 but the older doorway survives). In the eighteenth century many of the present buildings appeared, including St James's Church which overlooked the north end of the town. Duke Street and Lowther Street are both handsome Georgian streets which merit a visit.

The improvements to the harbour went hand in hand with the exploitation of coal. The poor natural inlet to the mouth of the Pow Beck was gradually improved, and by 1750 the Inner Harbour was protected. The numbers of ships registered at Whitehaven rose rapidly, and by

Whitehaven. Sir John Lowther laid out the new town in the 1660s having built the harbour for exporting coal. The grid pattern of his new town shows up clearly, although many additions were made to the town by the Lowther family in the eighteenth century. A coal mine lay on the south shore of the harbour. In the nineteenth century the railway linked Whitehaven with inland markets.

1790, 216 were listed – as many as at Maryport, Workington and Harrington put together.

The Lowther family prospered and built their 'castle' as a modification of the earlier Flat Hall; it is now Whitehaven Hospital. Mathias Reed, a local painter, established his reputation by painting its interior and that of St Nicholas's Church. Public buildings were built in the new town, a Poor House in 1743, a Dispensary (early hospital) in 1703, and the Market Place was extended in 1764. So Whitehaven was very much a town of the eighteenth century and one depending on the wealth of the Lowthers (later the Earls of Lonsdale). Other benefactors appeared and several schools were founded in the early nineteenth century: Matthew Piper, a Quaker, founded the Marine School in 1817 and a National School was built in 1814.

The population of Whitehaven soared in the eighteenth century. It was estimated in 1713 at 4,000, and in 1801 it was 17,000 (the figure for 1971 was 26,714). The arrival of the railways at Whitehaven in the nineteenth century reduced the port's sea trade apart from that to Ireland. Then the production of the Cumberland Coalfield fell away steadily during the nineteenth and twentieth centuries, and now there are no pits working near Whitehaven. As one stands on the quays today, it is difficult to visualize the once-bustling harbour.

The Curwen family of Workington Hall had held land in the region from the twelfth century and when the coal under their estates began to be exploited in the seventeenth century, their fortunes rose. Like the Lowthers at Whitehaven, the Curwens laid out a new section of the town, of which Portland Square was to become the focus. A new market was created and by 1829 the town had a National School and Assembly Room.

Maryport grew up at the mouth of the River Ellen. In 1749 the small harbour was built by Humphrey Senhouse and the new town laid out on the hill above the harbour. The bridge crosses the River Ellen which flows from right to left. The old houses beyond the bridge have been turned into a small maritime museum.

Workington became the northern centre of the west coast iron and steel industry. Railways linked it with Durham coking coal and with iron ore mines, both in the limestone belt which stretched from Egremont to Rowrah, and with those in the slate regions at Beckermet and at Murton and Ketton Fells. It became the most industrialized of the west coast ports.

Further north is the attractive little port of Maryport which prospered in the eighteenth century in the hands of the Senhouse family. Before the town expanded, the River Ellen reached the sea at the hamlet of Ellenfoot. In 1749 Humphrey Senhouse had an Act of Parliament passed to allow the river mouth to be widened and a new pier to be built, and by 1774 it was noted that there were wooden piers and quays all along the river. As ships got bigger the surviving Maryport yards had to launch ships side-on into the river west of the Motte. In the nineteenth century Maryport became famous for its Holme Line clippers. In the nineteenth century two docks were built: Elizabeth Dock in 1857 and Senhouse Dock in 1884; large rail yards were laid out to serve those docks and the port reached its peak of coal exports and iron ore imports in about 1900. After a brief revival in World War II the port has declined as the collieries have closed. As well as the quays and harbour, the little eighteenth-century town built by Humphrey Senhouse is worth visiting; the best view of the town is from Motte Hill.

Industrial and Market Towns

Ulverston is the major market town of Furness, having superseded Dalton-in-Furness after the Dissolution of Furness Abbey in 1534. It lies against the southern edge of the Silurian rocks on the lower limestone on the belt of sheltered farmland that skirts the northern edge of Morecambe Bay. Its history contrasts with that of the three coal ports but it too bears the stamp of the eighteenth century in its buildings and in the changes that it underwent.

It has a Norman parish

church, much rebuilt in 1805 and again in 1864–66, and it received a market charter from King Edward I in 1280. The market cross stands at the crossing of the coast road with the road from the fells, in an attractive market place flanked by eighteenth-century limestone buildings. In 1805, the author of the earliest guide to the Lakes, Thomas West, commented that it was too small a market place for all the business transacted there. He made the slightly ambiguous comment on the town that 'the wealthier inhabitants are polite, the tradesmen civil and many of them respectable'.

In an attempt to retain the town's role as a port, especially for the export of iron ore, a canal was built in 1796 to give better access to the open bay, and a new canal quarter was constructed to the south-east of the town. Unfortunately the channel of the River Leven shifts frequently and so access to the canal entrance has always been difficult. The construction of Barrow docks in the 1870s reduced Ulverston's trade and its population graph is a very different one from those of the industrial iron and steel towns. The main exports from Ulverston were iron ore from the quarries in the limestone area and slate from the Kirby Ireleth quarries owned by the Dukes of Devonshire. By the 1850s there were two iron foundries, two cotton mills, a linen works and a rope factory, as well as the workhouse and gas works that would be expected of a country market town. A fine viewpoint of the town is from the Barrow Monument on Hoad Hill, which was built in 1850 in memory of Sir John Barrow, an Ulverston man, a famous explorer and Secretary to the Admiralty.

Wigton, once the centre of a barony of the same name, is the main market town of the Solway Plain. It was tidied up around 1800 following criticism of the way the shambles (meat market) spoilt the market place. Parson and White in their *History and Gazetteer* of 1829 noted that 'a spacious square laid out with an ornamental cast iron pump in its centre' had replaced the older layout.

Wigton became a fast-growing textile-making centre after 1750. Formerly it was famed for its linen yarn and fabrics but by the end of the eighteenth century these were giving way to cotton manufacture and to an important calico printing firm. There were also the usual rural industries, including several breweries and tanneries and hat, nail and soap makers. The town's population trebled between 1790 and 1821, but there were still great stretches of common land around it until they were finally enclosed in 1801. Between two and three thousand sheep grazed these commons as did, by the end of the eighteenth century, increasing numbers of Scottish Galloway cattle.

Interestingly, W. Hutchinson in his *History of the County of Cumberland* (1794) mentions that there were still a few clay houses, implying that once there had been more, and emphasizing that the use of building stone was a fairly recent innovation for the smaller buildings.

In the south-east corner of Cumbria are three other small market towns: Kirkby Stephen, Kirkby Lonsdale and Sedbergh. Kirkby Stephen lies along the west bank of the River Eden at the mouth of the Vale of Mallerstang. Its market dates from 1352 and nothing earlier than thirteenth-century work survives in the big sandstone church. As at Sedbergh, its Grammar School, which was founded in 1556, was linked by scholarships to St John's College, Cambridge, to which a steady flow of Cumbrians had gone including Wordsworth, who went from Hawkshead Grammar School. Defoe noted that Kirkby Stephen was the centre of a stocking-knitting area and by the end of the century there were several textile mills in the little market town.

Kirkby Lonsdale overlooks the fast-flowing River Lune and is linked to Lancashire by the famous fifteenth-century Devil's Bridge. Its Norman church was described by Pevsner as having the 'most powerful early Norman display in Westmorland (or Cumberland) and the town is therefore worth a visit for its church alone.' He went on to say: 'It is a town of dark grey stone houses, enjoyable to wander through and indeed nowhere not enjoyable.' It has a variety of attractive town houses ranging in date from the seventeenth to the nineteenth century, all of which have used the local limestone as the major building material; much rebuilding took place in the late eighteenth century. The views from the town are as good as the town itself. Kirkby Lonsdale was given its market in 1227 and its Grammar School in 1591 which, together with Kendal School, was endowed with scholarships to Queen's College, Oxford.

Sedbergh is the third of this trio of market towns and the smallest. It is beautifully situated at the foot of the Howgill Fells above the River Rawthey. Like both Kirkbys it was important for its stocking-making, and by the early nineteenth century Sedbergh had two cotton mills. It is best known for its famous Grammar School, now an independent school. Founded by Roger Lupton, a benefactor of the original foundation of St John's College, Cambridge, it was endowed both with fellowships and scholarships to St John's. It was the greatest single source of undergraduates at St John's during the century 1661–1765.

Events at Sedbergh in the eighteenth century reflect general processes that were occurring throughout the region as the Lake District was drawn into the wider English cultural scene. To this period also belong the gradual civilizing of great areas of common and waste on the Cumbrian Lowlands, and the growth of a new industrial area based on the Cumberland Coalfield.

THE NINETEENTH CENTURY

The population of Cumbria has grown far less quickly than that of most of the other regions of England. From 1801 (when the first census was taken) to the beginning of this century England's population increased by 515 per cent whereas Cumberland's population increased by 220 per cent and Westmorland's by 155 per cent. Moreover, the rural areas have suffered quite dramatic losses of population: the isolated valley of Longsleddale, for example, had 187 people in 1801, 170 by 1851, 144 in 1901 and 101 by 1921; and in north-west Cumberland, Lorton township had 298 people in 1801, 449 in 1851, 326 in 1901 and 265 in 1921. These figures show a typical pattern of population change as the increasing numbers of surviving children had to leave to seek work outside their native valleys.

The major population trend of nineteenth-century England was the rapid expansion of the industrial towns. The making of iron and steel and the growth of engineering were the foundations of this pattern, while the cotton and woollen industries, which had already developed, continued to expand throughout the century. England became a country of townspeople to such an extent that the search for peace and quiet and escape from the towns was to become the major twentieth-century force at work on the Lake District.

Until about 1851 most villages did expand, but by then their capacity to absorb an increasing population had peaked. Manufacturing industry slowly

The Spinnery, Bowness, c.1900. Spinning, weaving and knitting have always been important Lake District crafts. Hand-spinning and weaving gave way to water-powered machines in the eighteenth century and later to steam power.

undermined many rural crafts, especially hand-loom weaving, brewing, corn milling, shoe-making, leathercrafts and so on. After about 1871 English agriculture, more especially arable farming, went into a decline as cheap foreign corn began to arrive from Canada, Australia, the United States and the Argentine. Corn-growing virtually disappeared from the Lake District, though the fertile Vale of Eden retained a more arable character. The now-disused corn mills of Ambleside and places such as Ulpha, in the Duddon Valley, all bear witness to this change.

The Cumbrian towns did not grow anywhere near as rapidly as the towns of South Lancashire or the Midlands. Carlisle, Kendal, Penrith and Appleby still look and feel like market towns. However, if one walks from Penrith Castle down into the town centre one sees some attractive nineteenth-century terraces between the railway station and the old town. Similarly, Carlisle has a railway town west of its medieval walls.

The outstanding industrial town of Cumbria was Barrow-in-Furness, the growth of which has been fully described by John Marshall in *Furness and the Industrial Revolution.* It did not exist until about 1850. Its population then was about 600 and it was merely a group of jetties for the export of iron ore. In 1859 the first blast furnaces came into production and Barrow burst into life, so that between 1864 and 1872 its population rose from 7,000 to 30,000, an increase of more than 400 per cent. By 1901 it had 57,000 people and was a major centre of iron and steel making and also shipbuilding. An entirely nineteenth-century town was laid out, initially to a town plan which was only partially completed.

On the far side of the Duddon estuary Millom underwent a smaller but similar pattern of growth and its population trebled between 1861 and 1871 after its iron works were built. The furnaces have closed and now Millom is a shadow of its former self.

Further up the coast the three eighteenth-century coal ports of Maryport, Workington and Whitehaven had less dramatic nineteenth-century stories. Ironically, the local coal was not a good coking coal and Barrow got its coke from Durham via the South Durham and Lancashire Union Railway.

Literary Visitors

By 1830 the literate and literary visitors, the painters, the printmakers and the publishers of guide books had put the Lakeland core of the region in the forefront of many cultivated minds. Of all those associated with

Sir George Beaumont (1753–1827), a wealthy landowner, amateur painter and one of the founders of the National Gallery. He was a friend and patron of Wordsworth and gave him a cottage near Keswick (which he never occupied). Sir George lived for a period at Old Brathay, near Ambleside, and bought the Loughrigg Tarn estate.

Top left: J. M. W. Turner (1775–1851), whose most famous painting of the Lakes is *Morning Amongst the Coniston Fells.*
Above: Patterdale Church and Ullswater Head, from Ackerman's *Picturesque Tour of the English Lakes* (1821). The view looks south to the Kirkstone Pass and Patterdale Hall, rebuilt by John Mounsey ('King of Patterdale') in 1820. The Marshall family bought the hall shortly after this picture was painted and began to plant trees on a large scale, giving the area the wooded appearance that it has today.

Top right: Calder Abbey, in an illustration by T. H. Fielding from Ackerman's *Picturesque Tour of the English Lakes* (1821). Originally a Savignac Priory founded in 1134, it united in 1148 with the Cistercians. The surviving work is largely Early English (thirteenth century).

the Lake District it was the Wordsworths and perhaps John Ruskin who had the greatest influence. Referring to Constable and Wordsworth, the art historian Kenneth Clark has pointed out the similarity of approach shown by painter and poet. He said: 'They were united by their rapture in all created things – Wordsworth's daisies and glow-worms, Constable's willow by the stream and the cottage in the cornfield.'

Constable visited the Derwent Water and the Borrowdale areas; his *Storm over Derwentwater, Evening* painted in 1806 is a soft, atmospheric painting that illustrates exactly the descriptive passages written by Dorothy Wordsworth and the poems of her brother. J. M. W. Turner also painted in the Lakes during the late 1790s and his *Morning Amongst the Coniston Fells* captures the atmosphere of the distant lake, clouds and fells.

Ackerman, in his *Picturesque Tour of the English Lakes* which was published in 1821, illustrated the Romantic approach to scenery: 'Here we have valleys of the utmost softness and beauty, luxuriantly wooded and watered by these enchanting lakes and the crystal streams which flow from them, deeply embosomed amidst lofty mountains, whose sides exhibit wild rocks majestically piled on each other, with yawning gulfs between, down which foaming torrents descend from dark and gloomy Tarns; and whose elevated summits sometimes peaked and sometimes running out into extensive ridges – enveloped in clouds and mists, appear in all the gloomy grandeur of the imagery of Ossian.' The hand-coloured prints by T. H. Fielding and J. Walton also capture this approach beautifully in the book.

In 1871 John Ruskin, described by W. T. Palmer as 'the greatest master of English descriptive prose', bought Brantwood on Coniston Water. He fought the coming of the railway to the Lakes and did not favour a mass influx of visitors to the area. Of the 'lower orders' he wrote: 'I do not wish to see them on Helvellyn when they are drunk.' Sadly Ruskin was mentally unstable in his later years at Brantwood and his influence as a critic declined after the famous trial in which he was found guilty of having libelled the painter James McNeill Whistler. He stayed in relative isolation at Brantwood, though 'punctiliously when the servant called "The sunset, Mr Ruskin", as if announcing a distinguished guest [he would go] out into the open and gaze at the streaks of Turnerian crimson in the sky over Coniston Water.' He spent the remaining years of his life after 1883 in a 'state of clouded peace'.

Canon Rawnsley, a close friend of Ruskin and co-founder of the National Trust, helped to form the Lake District Defence Association, established in 1883. The proposed construction of a railway up Ennerdale and the enlargement of Thirlmere as a reservoir were major threats which urged its foundation. John Walton has analyzed the first 600 hundred members of this new society: fewer than 10 per cent were based in Cumbria. The list included 40 professors, 60 clergymen and 34 public schoolmasters, also many Leeds and Manchester merchants.

John Ruskin (1819–1900) and Holman Hunt (1827–1910) in the garden at Brantwood, Coniston. Ruskin, arbiter of aesthetic taste in the late nineteenth century, lived at Brantwood on Coniston

Expansion in Carlisle

Medieval Carlisle was a combination of fortress, cathedral city and market. It was famous for its annual hirings of labourers and for the flow of Scottish black cattle that entered England via this important droving centre. W. Hutchinson gives an excellent account of the city as it was at the end of the eighteenth century. He attributed the real upswing in Carlisle's industrial growth to the building of a new military road and turnpike to Newcastle. This was followed by the development of linen and cotton mills, and in 1756 a brewery was built. In 1761 calico printing was introduced and by 1797 about one thousand workers were employed at four printfields. This led to the evolution of subsidiary industries such as a soapery and of service industries such as Forster's Bank. In a cameo of the story of the Industrial Revolution nationally, Hutchinson showed how Scottish and Irish labour flowed into the town and how a rural family could earn twenty to thirty shillings a week in such factories instead of eight shillings on the land. Esquires began to deem it respectable to engage in commerce and trade. These new industrial premises were open to visitors and became a 'sight the traveller should not omit', with so many unfamiliar processes on view.

In 1829 the town had eleven cotton mills powered by five water wheels and six steam engines, ten gingham and check makers, two bleacheries, two calico printers, five dye-houses, three linen mills and a woollen mill and eight hat-makers. As well as textile mills there were six corn mills, four iron and brass foundries, eight nailworks and four tanneries. The waters of the Rivers Caldew and Petterill were reported to be especially good for bleaching cloth, though their tremendous potential energy was still underused.

By the 1790s, local coal was being mined from pits on land owned by the Earl of Carlisle at Blenkinsop, Talkin and Tindale Fells: it was sold by the cartload in Carlisle and by dealers at 5d 'the Carlisle peck'. Peat was brought into Carlisle from Scaleby and Rowcliff Mosses at ten peats a penny.

In 1823 a canal from Bowness-on-Solway to Carlisle was opened for ships of up to 100 tons. Over eleven miles long with eight locks, it ended in Caldewgate on the

Water until his death. He was a major influence in the founding of the Lake District Defence Association.

west edge of Carlisle. It had been proposed to continue the canal to Newcastle, but 117 costly locks would have been needed. In 1829 the railway was already being discussed as a better way of linking Newcastle with Whitehaven's West Indian trade, with an offshoot line to link Penrith to Ullswater and so carry slates from that area for building in Newcastle. There is no map evidence of the canal surviving on the present 1:50,000 OS sheet, but the now-derelict Carlisle-to-Port Carlisle railway used the former route of the old canal.

The building of the railways contributed enormously to the growth of Carlisle. The new lines linked the town first with Newcastle, then with Maryport, Scotland and the South. Their arrival was followed by a search for an improved port, first by building the line to Port Carlisle and later to Silloth. This led to the development of Silloth in 1857. Last to be built was the Midland line via Appleby along the system of expensive tunnels and viaducts through the Pennines to Hellifield. The network of railways led to more industry and much nineteenth-century terrace housing. Only Barrow shows a more dramatic growth pattern than occurred at Carlisle.

Railway Connections

Penrith is, like most of the Cumbrian towns, a medieval burgh. Its Castle is still a distinctive landmark on the western edge of the town next to that other great landmark of many successful towns: the railway station. Below and to the east of the Castle lies the main north-south axial street of the town, with some very fine buildings such as the handsome eighteenth-century parish church which is set within a square of earlier buildings, with the Mansion House on its east side. The River Eamont carries the water from the north-eastern valleys of the Lakes and lies just to the south of the town; two small tributaries of the Eamont provide a water supply for the town.

The railway arrived in 1846 and an important livestock market was set up between the Castle and the railway. This led to some growth of the town and a pleasant formal square was built off Brunswick Road; a new suburb was laid out east of the main north-south axis of Stricklandgate–Duke Street–Middlegate. This suburb had a new parish church, Christ Church, built to serve it in 1852. The George Hotel, part rebuilt, part original, was a headquarters for Bonnie Prince Charles during the 1745 Rebellion.

Appleby, the county town of Westmorland, is the old centre of a barony bearing its name and is a beautiful little market town, the sandstone buildings of which give a deceptively eighteenth-century appearance to what was a New Town laid out in about 1100 after Ranulph de Meschines had built his strategically sited castle there. The Scots under William the Lion burnt the town in 1174 and the castle was then strengthened by walling the bailey, and the beautifully sited Church of St Lawrence was also rebuilt. In 1179 Appleby received its first borough charter.

The importance of a family to the history of a borough is well illustrated by the role of the Cliffords who held Appleby from the late thirteenth century until 1675. The most famous Clifford was the last Lady Anne, who restored the Castle and built the charming group of almshouses outside the castle gates and added a new chancel to St Lawrence's Church.

Old Appleby probably existed before the new town was laid out because St Michael's Church in Bongate has a north doorway which

Until the arrival of the railway at Kendal in 1846, travellers depended on horse and waggon. Here Thomas Rowlandson (1756–1827) captures a Kendal scene in 1820.

may be Saxon and uses a Saxon hogback gravestone as a lintel. Unlike Carlisle, Appleby has remained essentially a market centre. In 1829 Parson and White commented that 'here are two extensive breweries and several manufacturers of smiths' bellows, but the town is principally supported by its market, fairs etc'.

The town's two railways were built later than many of the others in the region, being opened in 18€2 and 1877. Perhaps by then the effects of building elsewhere had mopped up industrial capital. The two stations lay side by side until the Beeching cuts to the rural network in the 1960s.

Kendal's full name is Kirkby Kentdale: 'the town with the church in the dale of the River Kent'. The earliest reference to the church was in the late eleventh century and it served a huge parish, reaching to the top of Dunmail Raise, eastwards to the Lune Gorge and westwards to the eastern shore of Windermere. Bowness and Grasmere parishes were carved out of this enormous parish in the sixteenth century. The big parish church of the Holy Trinity has work of the thirteenth century in it but the date of its predecessor is not known.

Kendal became industralized in the nineteenth century and has become residential in the twentieth. With its dark slate buildings it can look sombre on a wet day, but its position by the fast-

flowing River Kent and its sinuous main street with many excellent seventeenth- and eighteenth-century stone buildings set around deep yards and narrow lanes, its handsome church and dominant castle motte, combine to make it attractive to visitors. The Abbot Hall Museum of Lakeland Life and Industry should not be missed; its collection of Lakeland paintings is especially good.

'Kendal green' was the product that Kendal was best known for. It was a coarse woollen cloth or 'drugget' dyed a dark green and used widely for clothing by the poorer people. The first reference to it was made in 1331 and it was frequently referred to in Shakespeare's plays. Later, Kendal cloth was referred to as 'cotton' (before the import of American cotton) and many dealers and finishers became wealthy men. It was still being made in the 1770s, when it was being exported to the Americas via Liverpool. Local wool was also used for knitting stockings, but this very important source of a second income disappeared when the British Army began to wear long trousers instead of knee breeches. Tanning was also an important industry. The hides of fell sheep and surplus cattle were tanned here and Kendal's surviving shoe factory is derived from this earlier industry.

The soft, swift-flowing water of the River Kent drove many water mills in Kendal and upstream. It powered early fulling mills for felting cloth and it was valuable in the nineteenth century for the paper-making industry that developed there using the soft, pure water.

Scottish and Lakeland cattle provided important items for Kendal's market, being first recorded in 1309, and corn from the Lowlands came northwards to it. The cloth could be moved by pack horse and R. S. Ferguson in his *History of Westmorland* gives a list of the teams of packhorses working Kendal in the mid-years of the nineteenth century.

	Horses
One gang of packhorses to and from London every week of about	20
One gang from Wigan weekly	18
One gang from Whitehaven weekly of about	20
From Cockermouth	15
Two gangs from Bernard Castle	26
Two gangs from Penrith twice a week, about 15 each gang	60
One gang, about 15, from Settle twice a week	30
From York weekly about	10
From Ulverston	5
From Hawkeshead, about 6 twice a week	12
From Appleby, about 6 twice a week	12
From Cartmell	6
Two waggons from Lancaster twice a week, computed at 60 horse load	60
Carriages two or three times a week to and from Milnthorpe, computed at 40 horse load	40
From Sedbergh, Kirkby Lonsdale, Orton Dent, and other neighbouring villages	20
	354

The first stage-waggons from London to Kendal, in the place of packhorses began 1757. The first post-chaise kept for hire in Kendal was in 1754, and the mail-coach began to run from Kendal to London in 1786.

As trade increased, so communications were improved. In 1819 the Preston – Lancaster canal was extended to Kendal. Ferguson commented: 'It discovered new channels of commerce, it brought that necessary commodity of manufacture, coal, at a cheaper rate; and . . . caused an increase of wealth and an increase of the working population and thus contributed at once all the means of commercial prosperity and public accommodation.' The canal basin at the head of the Kendal Canal was brought right up into the town and this compares with the railway which in effect missed Kendal, and created the little junction settlement of Oxenholme. Kendal was only served by the Windermere branch line; it was originally intended that this line

Top: Allonby was one of a number of Cumbrian coastal resorts that was developed for sea-bathing in the early nineteenth century. It lost ground after the railway reached Silloth in 1856.
Above: The steam boat *Gondola* on Coniston Water, c.1880. The boat has been restored by the National Trust and is now sailing again.

would continue beyond Windermere and climb over Dunmail Raise to Keswick.

Here we must leave the major towns of the region. A number of small towns that grew because the railway gave them wider links can be mentioned more briefly. Some of them offer surviving stretches of interesting line that can be a welcome change from car-ridden roads. Shap summit, once a steam enthusiasts' mecca, is still a dramatic route. The coast line beginning at Carnforth, crossing the sands at Arnside viaduct and running round the edge of Furness, is another attractive route and from it two independent offshoots survive, one to Lakeside leading to the Windermere steamers, and the other from Ravenglass giving a scenic run up to Boot in Eskdale.

Top: The Windermere steam ferry, c.1905. This linked the railhead at Windermere with the west side of the lake and the head of the lake.
Above: Derwent Water in winter, when the Lake District reverts to being the home of its natives for a few months.

Resorts such as Arnside, Grange-over-Sands, Seascale, Sellafield, St Bees and Silloth all shared in the railway boom, or indeed were virtually created by the railway. Inland, Windermere, Ambleside and Keswick were the main tourist centres of the Lake District. Keswick has already been described as a mining centre, but Windermere was entirely a railway creation. It was merely the hamlet of Birthwaite in the old parish of Bowness until 1847, when the Lake was linked with London almost at the time when the main line was built through Oxenholme to Carlisle. In 1821 Ambleside was described as 'a long rambling awkward town, pleasantly situated among woods of all kinds'. However, if one stands on Todd Crag or on Wansfell Pike and looks down on Ambleside, it composes itself very well. The route up Stock Ghyll offers glimpses of the older buildings and higher up the track the views of Langdale are superb. The upper part of the town around the old Church of St Anne (built in 1802) and the manor house is the least spoilt part of Ambleside.

The Armitt Library of Local History, a part of the town library, is well worth bearing in mind for a wet day: it has a very comprehensive collection of Cumbrian material. *The Lake Counties from 1830 to the Mid-Twentieth Century*, by John Marshall and John Walton, is the fullest account of the region written recently which covers the nineteenth and twentieth centuries.

Top: Cockling at Grange-over-Sands. It is still possible to follow the ancient trackway across the sands as far as Hest Bank, near Morecambe – though the authorities now insist that a local guide goes along too.
Above: Market place, Ambleside, by John Harden. This is probably an early nineteenth-century work.

CUMBRIA TODAY

A number of major recent changes have affected the appearance of the Lake District, some of which have their roots in the nineteenth century. Wordsworth might still recognize the Grasmere area and from the top of Loughrigg the views have changed very little. He would not, however, recognize the new lake of Thirlmere. He would find the new housing estates and the new road systems of Ambleside very confusing and it is unlikely that he would approve.

The motor car has greatly increased the numbers and types of visitor, and the daytrippers and coach parties have added their numbers to those of the conventional holidaymakers. New tourist attractions have been provided for the additional thousands: new affluence has meant more boats on the lakes, second homes at the ends of faster roads, and a multiplicity of new amenities for visitors to go to; some are a welcome addition, and others spoil the landscape. Today's planners in the Lake District have an obligation to try and harness the attempts to exploit the region's popularity.

The Great Conifer Debate

The first big debate about the nature of the Lake District landscape, and one which remains highly controversial, came with the large-scale planting of conifers, especially the larch. Wordsworth said quite firmly: 'It is therefore impossible, under any circumstances, for the artificial planter to rival the beauty of nature. But a moment's thought will show that if ten thousand of this spiky tree, the larch, are stuck in at once upon the side of a hill they can grow up into nothing but deformity: that while they are suffered to stand, we shall look in vain for any of those appearances which are the chief sources of beauty in a natural wood.'

Wordsworth did not condemn afforestation completely: while he pleaded for indigenous English trees to be allowed to regenerate naturally in the lowlands of the region, he was prepared to accept that 'there is so much barren and irreclaimable land in the neighbouring moors' where they could put 'their vegetable manufactory'. The section of his *Guide* on planting is well worth reading.

Some landowners had begun ornamental and commercial planting in the early nineteenth century, and the Marshall family in particular planted heavily around Patterdale and Coniston. Interestingly, the National Trust has now several old larch plantations under its wing; the surviving trees have acquired a variety of shapes, so avoiding the boring uniformity that Wordsworth deplored.

It was the construction of reservoirs, and with them the large-scale planting of evergreen conifers, that triggered off a major aesthetic argument. This reached its peak when Manchester Corporation planted the whole area around Thirlmere with conifers, especially Sitka spruce, primarily in order to hold the steep hillsides above their new reservoir in place and stop the rapid run-off, erosion and resultant infilling of the new lake. As one stands at the National Trust viewpoint near Thirlspot it is worth remembering that much of the view has been created within the last hundred years and it is clear that woodland management has progressed a long way from the earliest days of mass planting with straight-edged forest plastered across the whole area. The nature trails laid out in these woods along the Lake's western shore also emphasize the change in approach to reservoir management that has taken place since the days when 'Keep Out' was the only sign to be seen in the area.

The most interesting area of afforestation is that of Grizedale Forest with its Grizedale Forest Park. This is a park run by the Forestry Commission but set within the National Park. Grizedale Hall was a nineteenth-century house in a landscaped park. The Forestry Commission bought the estate in 1937 for commercial planting and gradually much of the area between Windermere and Coniston was planted. The Forestry Commission began an experiment in opening up its woodlands and in explaining them to the public, partly by means of a museum and partly by developing nature trails and the nine-mile-long Silurian Way–a forest walk. This is a very worthwhile way of finding out a great deal about an interesting part of the Lake District and offers a contrast

Above: Indigenous Lake District oak wood, Borrowdale.
Left: In the first phase of conifer planting in the Lake District, ornamental larch was favoured. Some survivors are seen here at Summers How, above Windermere.

to a day on the high fells.

The Forestry Commission has established similar facilities in Thornthwaite Forest, near Keswick, from which splendid views of Bassenthwaite Lake and Skiddaw can be seen. In the extreme north of Cumbria, between the Liddel Water and the Black Lyne, lies Kershope Forest Park. In the Eden Valley there are two smaller forests, one near Greystoke and the other four miles south-east of Penrith at Whinfell Forest. Ennerdale and the Duddon Valley have also been widely planted during this century. All these areas have plant and animal habitats not to be found on the unforested open fells, although in comparison, the plantations are biologically impoverished environments.

Some small areas of indigenous and near-indigenous woodland have survived. There are patches to be found on the slopes above the east shore of Coniston Water. Glencoyne Wood, just to the north of Glenridding, is a National Trust property, and on the other side of Ullswater is Hallin Fell Wood. On the east side of Haweswater is the isolated and beautiful Naddle Forest in which red deer may be seen. It is thought that some small areas of sessile oak wood may be survivals of the original forest cover; two famous examples are those at Keskadale and Birkrigg in Newlands Valley west of Keswick. Rowan often occurs in these woods too.

Borrowdale has many surviving areas of scattered oakwood with rowan, hazel and birch as subsidiary species as well as its famous ancient yews. Most of this woodland has recovered from having been coppiced for charcoal. Grizedale Forest has some lovely stretches of deciduous woodland amongst the newly planted conifers.

Alder grows well in wet land and is found on lake-head deltas and stream courses. In Martindale, east of Ullswater, alder woodland exists at between 900 and 1100 ft (275 and 335m), and as red deer will not touch alder there may be a selective process at work on these woods.

Finally, the dry, shallow limestone soils of the southern edge of the Lake District give rise to ash and hazel woods with some elm, oak and lime. Areas such as Yewbarrow, Whitbarrow and Underbarrow, and the country behind Arnside and Silverdale have stretches of these distinctive woods. There are also superb views of the Lakes, fells and Morecambe Bay from the crests of these limestone fells.

Building the Reservoirs

A second major change to the Cumbrian landscape has stemmed from the increasing demand for water supplies for the urban areas of industrial Lancashire. Manchester's demand for water trebled between 1851 and 1864 and the Corporation began to look at the cheap, clean supplies of water in the wet, sparsely peopled Lake District. There was strong opposition from the Lake District Defence Association, the national press and local MPs. The Act of Parliament was passed in 1879 and in 1885 Thirlmere dam was completed. The old Ambleside–Keswick turnpike had to be replaced and a new road was built along the west side of the expanded lake. Several farms including the Post Office at Waterhead were drowned. Manchester bought the whole catchment area for Thirlmere and began to plant the woodland already mentioned. The whole scheme has in recent years been made much more accessible to the public.

Haweswater was the next lake which Manchester looked at and, in that it was rather off the tourist track, the scheme had less opposition than that created by Thirlmere. A high dam was built and as a result the chapel and hamlet of Mardale were drowned. Another new road had to be built along the steep eastern side of the lake.

The coalfield towns also needed water, and Seathwaite Tarn, in a fine glacial corrie on the north side of Coniston Old Man, had its water level raised to supply these towns. Ennerdale Water has also been tapped, and even Windermere now contributes to Manchester's water supply. Wet Sleddale, north-east of Kendal, is the latest valley to have been commandeered for a reservoir and other eastern Lakeland valleys have also been coveted and inspected by urban authorities eager for water. Several other small lakes and tarns have been used to provide a regular head of water for mining activities: examples are Levers Water on Coniston Old Man and the bleak reservoir at the head of Kentmere.

Thirlmere as sketched by Edward Lear.

The first major conifer plantations were those planted round the new Thirlmere reservoir by Manchester City Waterworks. This development was strongly opposed by the newly formed Lake District Defence Association.

Tourism and the National Park

As well as new woods and more and bigger lakes, the third impact of this century on the Cumbrian landscape has been that of tourism and its

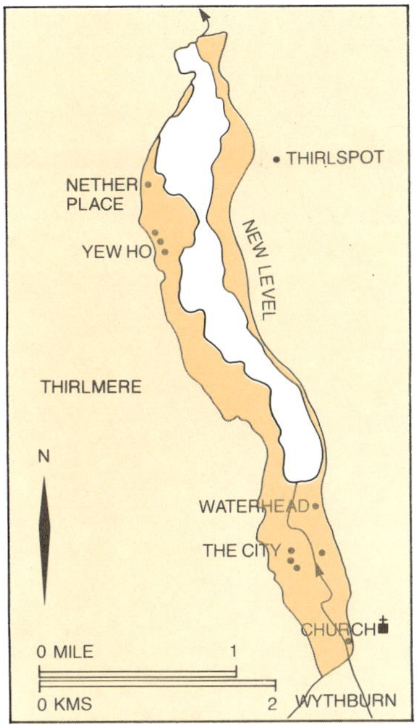

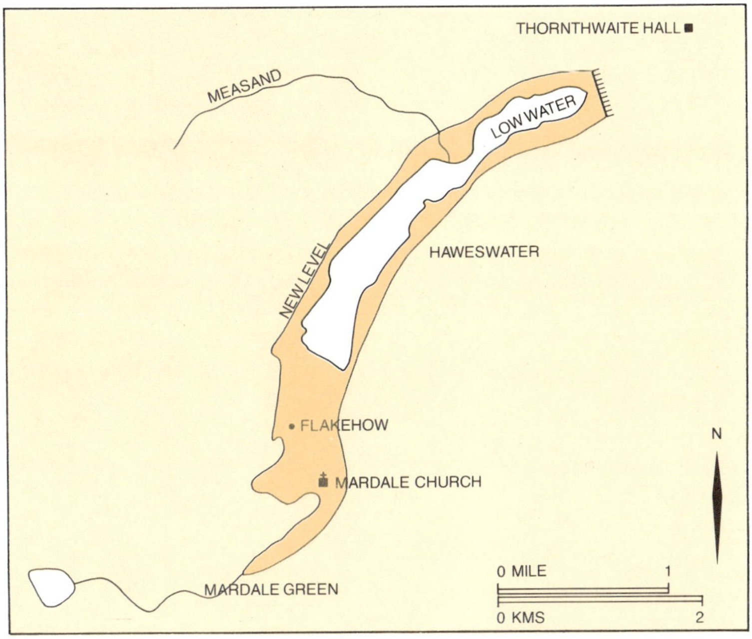

Top: Man has altered the shape of Thirlmere since it was sketched by Edward Lear in 1836, and that of Haweswater, as the industrial towns reached out into the mountains for new water supplies.
Above: The second major reservoir was built at Haweswater. Mardale village was drowned. This view looks south to Gatescarth Pass and Harter Fell.

related phenomenon of improved roads for the car-borne tourist. There have been major modifications in the road system in the last twenty years. The construction of the M6 reduced the effective distance of the Lake District from Lancashire, Yorkshire and the Midlands. This greatly increased the traffic arriving at Ambleside and also the accessibility of Ullswater and Haweswater. The improvements in the A55 from Scotch Corner via Penrith to Workington have made Keswick more accessible; the main aim of the latter improvements was, however, to try to improve communications for industry in the declining coalfield towns. The A590 to Barrow from Levens Hall has also been much improved but it is still a tortuous route and always will be. Dramatic schemes for a Morecambe Bay barrage, freshwater storage reservoirs behind it, and a motorway to Barrow from Morecambe along the top of the barrage seem to have disappeared, at least for the time being.

The creation of a National Park was another important development in the evolution of a part of Cumbria. The Lake District National Park was opened in 1951. In so far as the Park Planning Committee merged a part of the powers of the pre-1974 Lancashire, Cumberland and Westmorland County Councils, it was a precursor of the new county of Cumbria, formed in 1974. Through its planning powers the

National Park Board has had several important effects. It channels government grants from the Countryside Commission to specific projects such as much-improved signposting and waymarking of footpaths. It exercises control over planning applications on buildings so that local building materials are used wherever possible, and schemes for caravan and camping sites are also monitored. Finally, the Park exercises an information and educational role by means of its Information and Educational Centre at Brockhole on Windermere and by its system of guides and wardens who both inform and help the thousands of visitors who come to the Park every year. From time to time the Park authorities even have to close footpaths and over-used sites in order to protect them. Tarn Hows, Dungeon Gyll and Loughrigg near Ambleside have all had to be rested in order that the public who want to enjoy sites such as these do not ruin them.

Country sports, fairs, Gypsy gatherings, shows and sheepdog trials are all indigenous to Cumbria and some 42,000 people work within the Lake District National Park–more than would do were it not a tourist area. The social effects are various: the sheep farmer may well sense, for example, that he

Brockhole National Park Visitors Centre. Built by a Manchester businessman, Brockhole is now the major National Park centre for introducing visitors to the Lake District with a wide range of exhibits and presentations.

could make more money with less effort were he to run a caravan site, and local people certainly find that houses cost them much more than they would were there no tourist industry. Almost certainly tourism brings more money to Cumbria, or at least to the Lake District, than farming would.

However, there are other trends: as the collieries close, as iron mining has finished and as more of Britain's ships are built abroad in places such as Korea, and railway lines are made in Poland, so the western edge of Cumbria has suffered. Workington, Whitehaven and Maryport have fewer people now than they had in 1961, as has Barrow. The balance of one area vis-à-vis another continues to shift. Where Vikings settled the coast, Cistercian monks tamed Furness and developed Dalton-in-Furness, and Dalton gave way to Ulverston; Millom has come, gone, come, and almost gone again. One hesitates to think what more leisure may mean for the region.

Natives of Cumbria, and those who consider themselves native, must have scant sympathy when they see the traffic in Ambleside and Keswick grind to a halt. And yet they can still enjoy the light on the lakes and the skylines of the fells: they at least do not change.

Sellafield (formerly Windscale) – a much-debated symbol of the twentieth century. The original nuclear power station was located here because the site was isolated and sea water was readily available for cooling and for waste disposal. This view is from the prehistoric Grey Croft stone circle.

ACKNOWLEDGMENTS

The publishers are grateful to Richard Muir who took most of the photographs. Other illustrations were kindly provided by:

Abbot Hall Museum, Kendal 46, *Kentmere Hall* (c.1816) by John Harden, M.V. Young Collection; 60 bottom, *The Slate Wharf, Clappersgate* (1810) by John Harden, M.V. Young Collection; 69 right; 74; 80, *The Kendal Flying Machine* (1820) by Thomas Rowlandson; 82 top, *Allonby, Cumberland* (1812) by John Harden, M.V. Young Collection; 82 bottom, 83 top, Walmsley Bros; 84 top, Joseph Hardman; 84 bottom, A.S. Clay Collection; 88 top.
J C Barringer 30 top; 37 top; 70; 72.
Cambridge University Collection of Air Photographs 31 right; 39; 49; 71.
Cambridge University Library R.A. Ackerman *A Picturesque Tour of the English Lakes* (1821) 36 bottom, 60 top, 67 top, 76 bottom, 77 top right.
Fitzwilliam Museum, Cambridge 37 bottom; 66 bottom.
Mansell Collection 38; 67 bottom; 68; 76 top left, J.M.W. Turner drawn by J. Gilbert, engraved by W.J. Linton; 78.
National Portrait Gallery 75, Sir George Beaumont by G. Dance (1807).
Trustees of Dove Cottage 69 left.
Tullie House Museum, Carlisle 29.
Victoria and Albert Museum 66 top.
Woodmansterne Ltd 90 left.
Maps and diagrams by Stephen Gyapay.

FURTHER READING

The Lake District contains much of pre-1974 Cumberland, all Westmorland and Lancashire north of the sands (Furness). Cumbria contains all of pre-1974 Cumberland, Westmorland, Furness and a small part of the north-western corner of the old West Riding of Yorkshire. There is therefore no simple guide to the bibliography of the larger area (Cumbria) or the smaller (the Lake District).

The starting point for Cumberland and Westmorland is the **Bibliography of the History and Topography of Cumberland and Westmorland** compiled by Henry W. Hodgson (1968). The two major early topographical histories are **The History and Antiquities of the Two Counties of Westmorland and Cumberland** by J. Nicolson and R. Burn 2 Volumes (1777) and W. Hutchinson's **History of the County of Cumberland** 2 Volumes (1794), reprinted 1974.

The major journal of the region, in which the articles range from archaeology through to every aspect of the history of the region, is the **Transactions of the Cumberland and Westmorland Antiquarian and Archaeological Society.** The three scholars who contributed many of the most important articles on every aspect of the history of the two counties were W.G. Collingwood between 1890 and 1930; H.S. Cowper between 1890 and 1932, and R.S. Ferguson from 1871 to 1896.

In 1894 Ferguson produced **A History of Westmorland** having compiled one of Cumberland in 1890. In 1925 W.G. Collingwood brought out his **Lake District History.** More recently W. Rollinson has produced his readable **A History of Man in the Lake District** (1967) followed by his attractively designed **History of Cumberland and Westmorland** (1978).

The natural environment has been of great significance in shaping modern Cumbria and the authoritative text that sets the physical and ecological scene for the region is **The Lake District** by W.H. Pearsall and W. Pennington (1973). The two major geographical studies, both by R. Millward and A. Robinson, are **Cumbria** (1972) and **The Lake District** (1974).

All the texts referred to so far open up many more references for the reader wishing to explore particular periods, places or themes in more detail, and below are some leads to the wealth of historical writing on the region.

Clare Fell has summarized the prehistory of the area in **Early Settlement in the Lake Counties** (1972) and Tom Garlick summarized the next phase with **Romans in the Lake Counties** (1970). There is no major study of the medieval period in Cumbria as yet but J.C. Atkinson's edited edition of the **Coucher Book of Furness Abbey,** published by the Chetham Society in 1886–87, is a veritable quarry for material of that period. The major study of the period after the Dissolution of the Monasteries is **The Lake Counties 1500–1830** by C.M.L. Bouch and G.P. Jones, and J.D. Marshall and J.K. Walton completed the story with **The Lake Counties: 1830 to the Mid Twentieth Century** in 1981. J.D. Marshall has produced several other important studies of Lakeland life in the nineteenth and twentieth centuries and the Centre for North Western History which he established at the University of Lancaster has triggered off much new work on the region.

Specific moments in the history of Cumbria and the Lake District are revealed by directories such as that for 1829 published by W. Parson and W. White under the title of a **History and Gazetteer of Cumberland and Westmorland** and by many guide books to the region. Of these **A Picturesque Tour of the English Lakes** (1821) by R.A. Ackerman and William Wordsworth's **Guide to the Lakes,** re-issued in 1977 edited by de Selincourt, are two outstanding examples. The **Journals of Dorothy Wordsworth** edited by Mary Moorman (1971) and T.W. Thompson's **Wordsworth's Hawkshead** (1970) give vignettes of the Lakes at an important stage of their history.

Particular themes or topics provide another starting point for reading about an area. W.T. Shaw produced **Mining the Lake Counties** (1970) and J. Postlethwaite's **Mines and Mining in the Lake District** (1877 and later editions) is the standard work on this theme. J.D. Marshall and M. Davies-Shiel have produced a comprehensive **Industrial Archaeology of the Lake Counties** (1969) and J.D. Marshall's **Furness and the Industrial Revolution** (1958) is a very detailed account of the development of the iron and steel industry of Furness and the growth of Barrow. The buildings of the region are very distinctive and N. Pevsner's two volumes, **Cumberland and Westmorland** (1967) and **North Lancashire** (1969) are the standard guides. R.W. Brunskill's **Vernacular Architecture of the Lake Counties** (1974) is the major study for those interested in local building styles and J.F. Curwen covered **The Castles and Fortified Towers of Cumberland, Westmorland and North Lancashire North-of-the-Sands** (1913).

There are many studies of individual parishes, churches and buildings. Three outstanding examples are given that show just what can be achieved in the detailed study of the history of localities. H.S. Cowper wrote a masterly study of **Hawkhead** in 1899; M.L. Armitt produced a study of **Rydal** edited by W.F. Rawnsley in 1916, and J.B. Bradbury has produced the latest full study in **A History of Cockermouth** (1981).

Maps Finally, no explorer should go without the Ordnance Survey's Landranger (1:50,000) or Pathfinder (1:25,000) maps, or the four special Outdoor Leisure maps of **The English Lakes.** Also published by the Ordnance Survey is an archaeological map of **Hadrian's Wall.**

INDEX

Page numbers in italics refer to illustrations.

A
Abbot Hall Museum, Kendal 41, 81
Ackerman, R.A.
 A Picturesque Tour of the English Lakes (1821) *76*, 77, *77*
Aethelfrith, King of Northumbria 32
Agricola, Julius 29
Aire Gap 32
Allen Bank, Grasmere *68*
Allerdale 35
Allonby 33, *82*
Alps, The 12, 13
Alston 18, 61
 Mines 55
Ambleside 11, 12, *28*, 29, 30, *30*, 31, *31*, 33, 47, 56, 61, 69, 75, 84, *84*, 85, 89, 91
 St Anne's Church 84
Ambleside to Keswick Turnpike 88
Appleby 19, 34, 35, 53, 64, 75, 79, 80, 81
 Barony of 35
 Castle 35, 79
 Churches 43
 St Michael's Church 34, 79
 St Lawrence's Church 79
Armitt Library of Local History, Ambleside 84
Arnside 19, 84, 88
 Viaduct 83
Ashness Bridge *12*
Askam 19
Aspatria 34
 Church 43

B
Backbarrow 60
 Iron Company 69
Bagot family 53
Bampton Grange 43
Banks, Abbot Alexander 41
Barnard Castle, Co Durham 81
Barnscar, Muncaster Castle 25
Barrow, Sir John 73
Barrow-in-Furness 19, *41*, 75, 79, 89, 91
Barrow Monument, Hoad Hill 73
Barton Church, Ullswater 43
Bassenthwaite Lake 16, 48, 87
Beaumont, Sir George *75*
Beckermet Fells, Thornhill 72
Bede's *Ecclesiastical History of the English Nation* 32
Beetham, Kendal 32
Bentham, Aire Gap 32
Bewcastle Roman fort 31, *31*
 Cross 33, 34
Bicknell, P. 64
Birdoswold, Gilsland 31
Birkrigg Forest, Newlands Valley 87
Birks Crag, Haweswater 27
Birley, Eric 32
Birthwaite, Windermere 84
Black Death, The 51
Blackpool, Lancs 11
Blea Water 16
Blencathra (Saddleback), Skiddaw 32
Blenkinsop Fells, Haltwhistle 78
Boot 83
Bootle 54
Bornby, Haweswater 33
Borrans Field, Windermere 30
Borrowdale 13, 16, *17*, 18, 20, 21, *21*, 27, *27*, 40, *66*, 77, 87, *87*
 Copper mines 61
Bowder Stone, Borrowdale *27*
 Quarry *62*
Bowland, Forest of 29
Bowness-on-Solway 29, 31, 78
Bowness Parish 80, 84
Bradbury, J.B.
 A History of Cockermouth 38, 57
Braithwaite, Edward 70
Brampton 56, 57, *57*
Branthwaite 48
Brantwood, Coniston Water 77, 78, *78*
Brathay, Ambleside 69, *75*
Bridekirk Church 43
Bridge House, Ambleside *63*
Bridget (Bride), Saint 43
Brigham 32, 48, 61
 Church 43
Brigwood, Brampton 57, *57*
British Museum, The 27
Brockhole Information & Educational Centre, Windermere 90, *90*
Brockstones Farm, Kentmere 47
Bromfield Church 43
Brotherilkeld, Eskdale 31
Brotherswater, Hartsop 69
Brough Castle 35, 36
 Roman fort 29
Brougham *28*, 29
 Castle 35, *37*, 38, *38*
Broughton-in-Furness *13*
 Manor 45, 53
Brown, Dr John 64, 66
Browne family 58, *58*, *59*
 George 58
Brunskill, R.W. 53
Burneside Hall 52
Burrow-in-Lonsdale 29
Buttermere-Loweswater Valley 48
Butts Beck Quarry, Dalton-in-Furness 27

C
Calder Abbey *77*
Caldew, River 31, 48, 61, 78
Calf, The, Howgill Fells 19
Cardew, Thursby 32
Carlisle 18, 19, 22, *28*, 29, 30, 31, 32, 33, *49* 53, 55, 64, 75, 78, 79, 80, 84
 Archaeological Unit 32
 Bishopric 48
 Caldewgate 78
 Castle 35
 Cathedral 48
 County of 35
 Diocese 48
 Earl of 78
 Forster's Bank 78
 Railway 79
 Rose Castle 48
 St Leonard's Church 43
Carnforth, Lancs 83
Carrock Fell 18, 27, *27*, 29, 32
Cartmel 35, 81
 Priory 19, 43
Castle Carrock 32
Castle Crag hill fort, Borrowdale 27, *27*
Castle Howard, N. Yorks
Castlerigg (Keswick Carles) 26, *26*
Castlesteads, Natland 27
Catterick, N. Yorks 29
Cautley Spout, Howgill Fells 19
Cavendish family 52
Chalk Beck, Skiddaw 55
Charles II, King 70
Charles, Bonnie Prince 79
Chester, Cheshire 29
Claude Lorrain 64
Claudius, Emperor 29
Clifford family 38, 79
 Lady Anne *36*, *37*, 38, *38*, 79
Coalbrookdale, Salop 60
Cocker, River 38, 64
Cockermouth 35, 48, *64*, *68*, 81
 Borough 48
 Castle 38, 48, 57
Cockleythwaite, Sebergham 33
Collath (Coalwith), Langdale 69
Collingwood
 R.G. 30
 W.G. 33
Colorado Desert 14
Colton parish 47
Coniston 20, 61
 Fells 61
 Old Man 88
 Valley *60*
 Water 12, 17, 40, 54, 60, 85, 87
Constable, J. 64, *66*, 77
 Storm over Derwentwater, Evening 77
Church Beck, Coniston 61
Clappersgate, Ambleside *60*, 69
Copeland
 Barony of 38
 Forest 55
Corbridge, Northumberland 29
Cotswolds, The 11
Countryside Commission 90
Crake, River 19
Croglam Castle, Kirkby Stephen 27
Croglin 67
Crosby Garret
 Church 43
 Fell 29
Crosby Ravensworth
 Church 43
 Fell 29
Crosscanonby 34
Cross Fell 14, 18
Crosthwaite, Kendal *53*
Crumnock Water *64*
Cumberland 11, 35, 52, 73, 74, 89
 Coalfield 72, 73
Cumrew 67
Cunsey Beck, Windermere 60
Curthwaite, Carlisle 33
Curwen family 70, 72
Curwen, J.F. 48

D
Dacre Church, Ullswater 43
Dacre family 57, *57*
Dacre, Sir Thomas 43
Dalston 32, 45
Dalton-in-Furness 41, 53, 72, 91
 Parish 47
Darby, Abraham I 60
Deadly Nightshade, Vale of, Furness 40
Dearham 32
de Barton, Robert 55
Defoe, Daniel 64, 73
de Fortibus, William 38
de Lyndeseye, William 48
de Meschines
 Ranulph 53, 79
 William 38
Dene, Cockermouth 48
Denson family 51
Dentdale 19
Denton Church, Upper Denton 43
Department of Environment 31
Derwent
 Fells 16, 32, 64
 River 16, 38, 48, *64*
 Water *12*, 16, 27, 77, *83*
de Vaux, Robert 43
Devil's Bridge, Lancs 73
Devoke Water 20, 22, 25
Devonshire, Dukes of 73
de Wint, Peter *37*
de Wra, William 51
Doble, Ralph 51
Domesday Book 35
Dove Cottage, Grasmere *68*, 69
Drigg 22
Duddon
 River 38
 Valley 18, 87
Dungeon Gyll, Great Langdale 90
Dunmail, King 35
Dunmail Raise 18, 47, *51*, 80, 83
Durham, Co. Durham 72, 75

E
Eaglesfield, Cockermouth 48
Eamont, River 29, *37*, 38, 55, 79
Easedale 21
Eden
 River 11, 18, 19, 31, *49*, 55, 64, 73
 Valley 14, 18, 19, 25, 26, *27*, 31, 32, 35, 64, 75, 87
Edmund, King 35
Edward III, King 55
Edward IV, King 55
Egremont 12, 35, 53, 72
 Castle 38, *39*, 44
Ehen, River 38
Ehenside Tarn 22
Ellen, River 72, *72*
Ellenfoot, Maryport 72
Elizabeth I, Queen 53, 61
Elterwater 20, *63*
 Common 21
 Quarries 63
Embleton Sword 27
Ennerdale 20, 78, 87
 Water 88
Esk, River 29, *30*
Eskdale 20, *31*, 32, 35, 40
Eskmeals, Newbiggin 22
Ewe Close, Crosby Ravensworth 27

F
Fairfield, Rydal Fell 55
Farrer, William *Records of Kendale* 48
Fell, Clare 26

Ferguson, R.S. *History of Westmorland* 81, 82
Fielding, T.H. 77, *77*
Finburg, Prof. H.P.R. 33
Fleming
Estate 55
Family 52
Flookburgh 54
Forestry Commission 85, 87
Fountains Abbey 40
Furness
Abbey 19, 31, 40, *41*, 42, 54, *54*, 56, 60, 72
Fells 21
Old Lancs 35, 40
Railway 60
Valley 26

G
Garrigill, Alston 55
Gatescarth Pass, Haweswater *89*
Gelt, River 57
Gilpin, Rev. William 66
Gilsland 35
Barony of 57
Glencoyne Wood, Glenridding 87
Goldscope Copper Mines, Keswick 55, 61
Gondola, Coniston Water *82*
Gosforth
Church 34, *34*, 43
Cross 34, *34*
Gospatric, Thomas 42
Grange-over-Sands 19, 84, *84*
Grasmere 47, 51, *51*, 54, 68, 80, 85
Chapelry 48
Marquis 'fee' 51
Richmond 'fee' 51
Parish 54
Parsonage *68*
Gray, Thomas *Journal of the Lakes* 66, *67*
Great Gable, Borrowdale 20
Great Mell Fell 25
Great Slack, Borrowdale *17*
Green, Stephen 69
Green, William 61
Greenburn Beck
Reservoir 61
Valley 61
Greenodd 19
Greta, River 16, 61
Greysouthern 48
Greystoke, Barony of 35
Greystoke Forest 14
Grige family 51
Grimston, N. Yorks 22
Grizedale
Forest 85, 87
Hall 85
Park 85
Gunnerkeld, Shap Fells 25

H
Hadrian, Emperor 29
Hadrian's Wall *28*, 31, *31*
Hallin Fell Wood, Ullswater 87
Harden, John 11, *84*
Hardknott, Upper Eskdale 29, *30*, 31, *31*
Hardknott Gill 31
Harington Man, Cartmel 43
Harrington 72
Harter Fell, Haweswater *89*
Hartrigg Farm, Kentmere 47
Hartsop 56
Haweswater 15, 27, 33, 88, 89, *89*
Hawkshead 33, 81
Courthouse 19, 41
Grammar School *68*, 73
Parish 47
Hellifield, N. Yorks 79
Helvellyn 13, *15*, *26*, 78
Henry I, King 35
Henry VIII, King 56
Heron Pike, Rydal Fell 55
Hesket Newmarket 54, 67
Hest Bank, Lancs *84*
Heversham 32
High Dale Park, Furness 41
High Furness Fells 40
High Kern Knott, Borrowdale *17*
High Pike, Rydal Fell 55
High Street, Roman road *28*, 29
Himalayas, The 12, 13
Hochstetter, Daniel 61
Holker Hall 43
Honister 20
Pass 61
Hoskins, Prof. W.G. 57
Howard family 52, 57
Howgill Fells 19, 73
Hunt, Holman *78*
Hutchinson W. *History of the County of Cumberland* 38, 73, 78

I
Ibbetson, J.C. 69
View of Castle Crag, Borrowdale *68*
Ickenthwaite, Coniston Water 60
Inglewood, Forest of 32, 35, 55
Ireby 54
Irish Sea, The *15*, 29, 70
Irthing
River 43, 57
Valley 31
Irton Cross *33*

K
Keld 43
Kendal 19, 53, *53*, 75, 80, 81, 82
Barony of 35
Canal 82
Grammar School 73
Holy Trinity Church 80
Market Place *53*
Parish 47, 48, *51*
Town Hall *53*
Kent, River 19, 45, 80, 81
Kentdale 19, 45
Kentigern (Mungo), Saint 43
Kentmere 21, 45
Green Quarter 46
Hall 46, *46*
Reservoir 88
Tongue House 46
Valley 63
Kershope Forest Park, Liddelwater 87
Keskadale Forest, Newlands Valley 87
Keswick 11, 16, 18, 66, *67*, 84, 89, 91
Copper Mines 61
Ketton Fells 72
King Arthur's Round Table, Eamont Bridge *24*, 25
Kirby Ireleth Quarries 73
Kirkbampton Church, Broughton-in-Furness 33, 43
Kirkbride 33
Church 43
Kirkby Lonsdale 19, 73, 81
Church 43
Grammar School 73
Market 73
Kirkby Stephen 34, 73
Church 43
Kirkby Thore Church 43
Kirkcambeck Church 43
Kirklinton Church 43
Kirkoswald Church 43
Kirkstone Pass 18, 55, 69, *76*
Quarries 63
Knipescar, Bampton 14

L
Lake District Defence Association 77, *77*, 88, *88*
Lake District National Park 85, 88, 89, 90
Lancashire 11, 32, 73, 75, 88, 89
Lancaster, Lancs 19, 81
Lanercost 43
Langdale Axe Factory 17
Langdale
Pikes 13, 18
Valley *12*, 13, 16, *16*, 18, 21, 51, 69, 84
Latrigg, Keswick *67*
Lawson Park, Furness 41
Lear, Edward *88*, *89*
Leath, Ward 35
Leven, River 19, 60, 73
Levens Hall 52, 89
Levers Water 61, 88
Lingmell Beck, Wasdale 51
Liverpool 11, 81
London Lead Company 61
Long Marton Church 43
Long Meg and her Daughters, Little Salkeld 26, *26*
Longsleddale 21, 46, 74
Lorton 74
Loughrigg, Ambleside *75*, 85, 90
Low Dale Park, Furness 41
Low Furness 19
Lowther 34
Lowther family 43, 70, *71*, 72
Christopher 70
Sir John 70, *71*
Lowther, River 42
Low Wray parish, Windermere 47
Lune
Gorge 80
River 11, 19, 29, 73
Valley 19, 26
Lupton, Roger 73
Lyttelton, Lord 66
Lyvennet Beck, Crosby Ravensworth 27

M
McCarthy, Mike 32
Malcolm I, King of Scotland 35
Mallerstang, Vale of, Kirkby Stephen 73
Mardale Forest, Haweswater 88, *89*
Malvern Hills 12
Manchester 11, 88
City Water Works *88*
Corporation 85, 88
Marron, River 48
Maryport 19, 31, 70, 72, *72*, 75, 79, 91
Elizabeth Dock 72
Maritime Museum *72*
Motte Hill 72
Quay 72
Senhouse Dock 72
Marshall family *76*, 85
Marshall, John *Furness and the Industrial Revolution* 75
Marshall, John and Walton, John *The Lake Counties from 1830 to the mid-twentieth century* 84
Masham, N. Yorks *68*
Martindale Forest, Ullswater 87
Mayburgh Henge, Penrith *24*, 25
Mickle Fell 18
Middle Dale Park, Furness 41
Middleton *28*
Milburn Church 43
Millom 19, 53, 75, 91
Millward, R. 61
Milnthorpe 81
Mindersdale Silver and Lead Mine, Upper Caldew Valley 55
Mite, River *30*
Morecambe 89
Morecambe Bay 11, *15*, 19, 72, 88, 89
Moresby, Whitehaven 31
Morland 33
Church 43
Mosedale Beck, Wasdale *51*
Mounsey, John 'King of Patterdale' *76*
Murton Fell 72

N
Naddle Forest, Haweswater 87
National Park Authority *19*
Natland 47
Naworth Park, Brampton 55, 57
Castle 57, *57*
Nenthead, Alston 61
Netherby 31
New Brighton, Merseyside 11
Newcastle 78, 79
Newlands Beck, Keswick 16
Newlands Valley Mines 61
New Park, Furness 41
Newton Arlosh 54
North Atlantic Ocean 12
North European Plain 12

O
Orton, Carlisle 32, 81
Orton, Tebay 81
Orton Fell 29
Oswald, Saint (King of Northumbria) 43, 48
Oughterby 33
Outward Bound 11
Oxendale, Langdale *12*
Oxenholme 82, 84
Oxen Park, Furness 41

P
Palmer W.T. 77
Papcastle 29, 32
Park-a-Moor, Furness 41
Park House, Furness 41
Parson, W. and White, W. *History & Gazetteer* 73, 80